Reaching Out to the Stars

American Idol Dreams

By Donna DeMaio Hunt

First Printing
Illustrations:
Critique:

ISBN 1463673574   Soft cover

If we all judged a book by its cover, we could only imagine what lies inside the journey of where a dream could take us.

Born and raised in Worcester, Massachusetts, I developed a great appreciation and love for music. I dreamed of spending my life as a vocalist but redirected my dreams in pursuit of a college degree and a career that was more promising. While attending Anna Maria College, I intended to graduate with a degree in English with the sole purpose of being a writer. I quickly became bored with literature classes, and changed my major. I graduated with a Bachelor's degree in Psychology in 1996, followed by a Master's degree in Counseling Psychology in 1998.

In 2000, I accepted a job in a junior/senior high school as a guidance counselor. I worked there for four years before becoming pregnant with my first child. After working with children and then raising my own, I began to revisit the roots of my passion: music and writing.

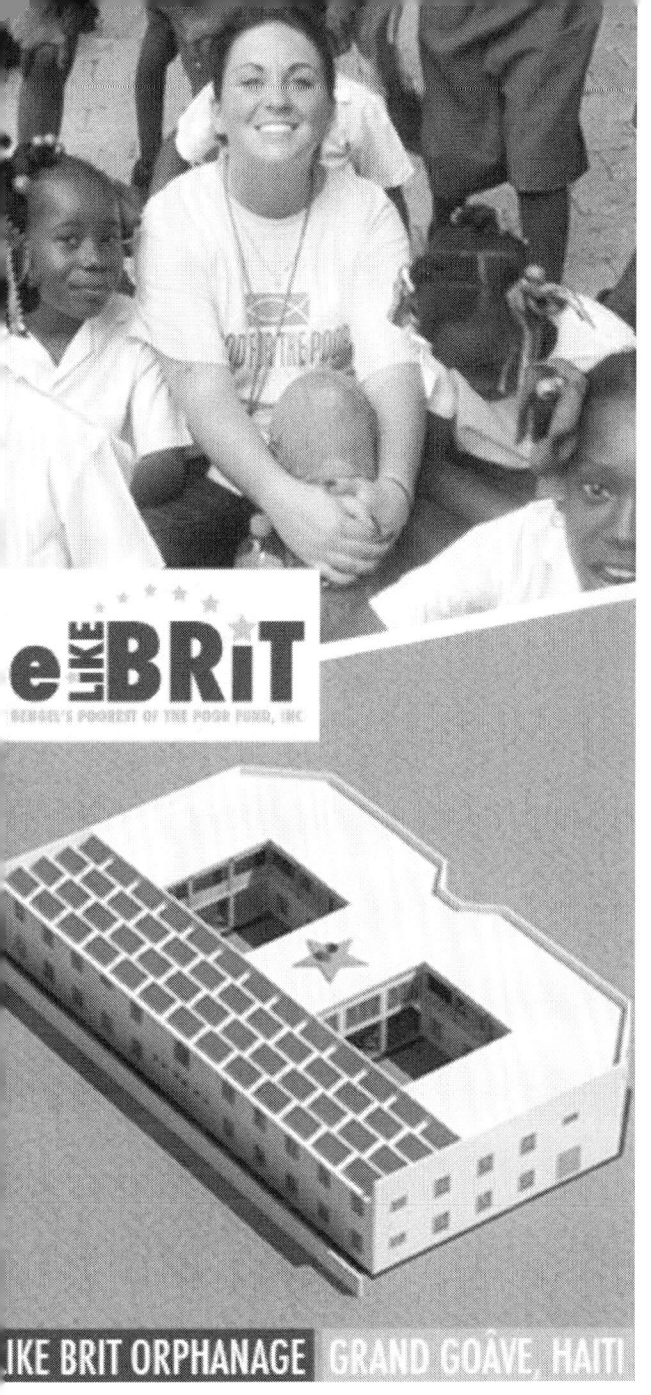

Be Like BRiT
GENGEL'S POOREST OF THE POOR FUND, INC.

LIKE BRIT ORPHANAGE GRAND GOÂVE, HAITI

With every purchase of *Reaching Out to the Stars (American Idol Dreams)*, a portion of the proceeds will be donated to Be Like Brit, Britney Gengel's Poorest of the Poor Fund, to build an orphange in Haiti. Britney was a resident of Rutland, Massachusetts, who lost her life in the earthquake that devastated Haiti in 2010. Britney was in Haiti volunteering her time to the children who had so little and needed so much. We should all strive to have a heart as big as Britney's and help to keep her dream alive!

5

Introduction

"My definition of an idol is not only someone you adore blindly and excessively, but someone you adore for one or more admired qualities, who you feel you have a connection with because of commonalities such as interests, morals and values."

~ Donna DeMaio Hunt ~

As a kid, being a fan is an act of innocence. We have dreams of being a famous rock star, a Hollywood actor or actress, et cetera. As we enter adulthood, we carry a piece of that inner child with us for always and forever. We wonder if as adults it's even normal or acceptable to have idols or crushes on certain celebrities. Although the stars have always had a great influence on my life, as a grown adult through fandom, my *American Idol* experience has influenced my life in many ways over the past eight years…

Contents

"Growing up, wanting to be a star or just meeting a celebrity of choice were two thoughts that have always followed me through life. I have never been able to fully let go of the challenge but sometimes on the way to a dream, you get lost and find a better one."

-Donna DeMaio Hunt-

You know a dream is like a river
Ever changing as it flows
And that dreamer's just the vessel
That must follow where it goes
Trying to learn from what's behind you
And never knowing what's in store
Makes each day a constant battle
Just to stay between the shores.

Too many times we stand aside
And let the waters slip away
'Til what we put off tomorrow
Has now become today
So don't you sit upon the shoreline
And say you're satisfied
Choose to chance the rapids
And dare to dance the tide.

And there's bound to be rough waters
And I know I'll take some falls
But with the good Lord as my captain
I can make it through them all.

Yes I will sail my vessel
'Til the river runs dry
Like a bird upon the wind
These waters are my sky
I'll never reach my destination
If I never try
So I will sail my vessel
'Til the river runs dry.

~ Garth Brooks ~

Dedication & Thanks

I dedicate this book to my husband Bryce, my best friend and my lifetime companion, who doesn't always get my quirkiness but puts up with it; for loving me unconditionally, when I'm at my best and most beautiful, my worst and ugliest; for not only loving me for my best qualities but for understanding that I, too, am subject to human error. I love you "Forever and for Always."

Special thanks to my wonderful husband, my two beautiful children, my loving and nurturing parents, my one and only talented brother and all of my family and friends who have supported me. I would also like to thank my famed favorites and *American Idol* for giving me the inspiration to write this book and to those of you who have touched my life somewhere along the way. Lastly, thank you to Erin Stelmach, Bonnie Beckeman and Winthrop Handy in helping to make this dream a reality.

"Being famous is just a job."
~ Britney Spears

**"I don't think I realized that the cost of fame is that it's
open season on every moment of your life."**
~ Julia Roberts

**"Acting is not about being famous, it's about exploring
the human soul."**
~ Annette Bening

Chapter 1
What Is A Star?

Jason Castro, his name printed on the door inside of a golden Hollywood star as I stood in front of his room. I was suddenly part of the top twenty- four finalists on the biggest reality television show ever, but ironically could not remember ever performing, not even once, in front of a crowd on stage. All I knew was that I needed to tell him how I felt because I somehow knew that my days there were limited.

The door was left slightly open as I heard the strumming of his guitar and his soothing voice rehearsing the song "Fragile" by Sting. As I walked into the room, he was sitting on the end of the bed. Wearing camo shorts and a gray t-shirt, a cross around his neck held by a gold chain, he never stopped strumming and continued to sing as he nodded me in.

I closed the door behind me and sat down in front of him, nothing separating us but an acoustic guitar. As I gazed into his blue eyes, I thought about getting up and running out the door as fast as my legs would carry me, but it was as if the connection was so strong that it enabled me to move from where I was sitting.

As I couldn't speak, before I could even think of what I would say or where I would begin, I silenced him with an unanticipated kiss. The strange thing was that as he reciprocated, and there was suddenly no longer a guitar separating us. I could still hear the music and his voice running through my mind as if there were a CD playing in the background.

As he placed his hand on the back of my head and gently laid me back on a pillow, his body slightly raised over mine, his lips moved from my mouth to my neck. As the electricity shot through me while his dreadlocks gently caressed my body, I felt a tugging on my right hand and a soft, sweet voice saying, "Mommy, is it time to get up yet? I'm hungry."

As I opened my eyes, my four year old son stood staring at me in his Batman pajamas. I said, "Alright honey, go ahead downstairs, I'll be right there." As I heard his little feet pitter patter down the stairs, I laid in bed for a moment. As I stared up at the ceiling, I thought to myself, what….the hell….is wrong with me?

I have never told that dream to anyone, but the answer to my question is *American Idol* overload.

As fans, we have thoughts that are embarrassing, feelings that we can't explain and questions that are never answered. We search for an answer to the question, "What is it that separates the world of Hollywood stars from their fans, the very people who put them where they are?"

What exactly is a star? The truth is that there are many different definitions: A celestial body visible at night from the Earth as relatively stationary, usually twinkling points of light; a graphic design having five or more radiating points, often used as a sign or merit of rank; an artistic performer or athlete whose leading role or superior performance is acknowledged; one who is highly celebrated in a field or profession; the future destiny.

I asked my best friend's daughter, Emma, age six, "What is a star?" She said, "Something in the sky that is really teeny, bright and yellow." Then I asked her mother, Maria, the same question and she said, "Hollywood people."

I have so many questions and so few answers. Let's start with why people in Hollywood are actually referred to as stars. Now, after knowing the definitions, is it because they are radiating, brighter and shinier than us, exposed to the world from every direction? Is it that they are of higher merit that they are considered to be above us? Is it because they are so far away that they cannot be reached? Is it that they live on their "own planet" or in another world that is unknown to most? Are they what we so frequently wish upon to be our destiny?

Of course, I am no different than any other, loving the entertainment industry; movies, television, music and even, at times, sports when I cannot rip the remote from my husband's firm grip. I am never stopping short of picking up a magazine with a famous face, wanting to know the scoop, tuning into talk shows and award shows, especially when they are hosted by Ellen DeGeneres or Billy Crystal. Oh, how I love the funnies.

What is not glamorous about the red carpet and the beautiful dresses?

Who didn't want Jennifer Aniston's haircut or Joey Tribiani for our best friend?

What guy would not want to be the teammate or peer of Tom Brady, now married to Gisele, who may have many hot friends? Or Big Papi, the power hitter of the one and only Boston Red Sox? And even the chair that sat J.Lo's butt at the *MTV Music Awards*?

How many desperate housewives would love to live on Wisteria Lane for just one day? Now there's some drama for you. You can't deny that their lives are far from boring.

How many girls would love to get the chance to be best friend's with Paris Hilton, or better yet, with Miley Cyrus?

How many millions of people want to be the next *American Idol*, as I would settle for just meeting one, preferably that of my selected fantasy boyfriends? We are all guilty of having the dream but why are we so different than those who get to live it? Of course, I've had the dream and some days still do as a mom who tucks her children into bed every night, knowing that they too will someday have the dream.

I find myself constantly struggling with the realities tied to being a devoted fan and living on the other side of the Hollywood splendor. In my thirty-six years here on this earth, the closest I have come to meeting one of my favorite celebrities is through my television, at a concert or in a dream. Meeting a celebrity of choice is something that has always been on my list of things to do before I die. There are many reasons why it is so important for me to meet my most admired stars. Therefore, I have never been able to let go of the challenge.

Everybody at one time or another in life finds themselves being some type of fan to one or more selected celebrities. As a child or young teen, it is somewhat expected. It is a fact that even as grown adults, we actually still carry a piece of that inner child.

My present experience with fandom as a grown adult stems from an addiction to the show *American Idol*. Watching the show has been a must since season two. For some reason, the excitement and pleasure the show has given me over the years has led me to never want to stop watching it from season to season, where missing an episode could be looked at as a complete and utter tragedy.

Being an *Idol* fan means more than being just a fan of the show and the chemistry of the judges. We become devoted fans of certain contestants, where the obsession never ends when a season ends but is long-lasting. When the show is over, we devoted fans will do anything in our power to follow them through magazine articles, websites, talk shows and not to mention the anticipation of their newly released   . albums followed by their tours. Every new season is a new adventure of finding a new love of our lives, whether we are single, in a relationship or married.

As the eighth season of *Idol* began, I remember the show replayed a memorable moment from season seven. As they were about to announce which of the two David's was to be the next *American Idol*, the cameras' focal point was on a group of young teenage girls anxiously awaiting the results. Clearly, David Archuletta fans, they went into total hysterics when the winner was revealed as David Cook. The screaming and crying was entertainingly humorous. What is more hysterical than the somewhat psychotic reaction from the young girls, is that we as adults tend to react the same way.

My experience focuses on my obsessions with contestants from three of the more talked about seasons. If you, too, are an *Idol* fan, you probably have experienced some of the same love, joy, excitement and even tears through the devotion of your most loved and admired *Idol* contestants.

Do celebrities really know what it is like to be a devoted fan? The answer to that question is yes. Sometimes they just lose sight of it. This is because everybody at one time in their lives is a die hard fan. That's right, it is true. Even celebrities are fans of other actresses and actors, musicians or sports figures. They have all once had an idol, someone they admire, and probably still do. I can assume for most celebrities that there was someone along the way who inspired them some time in their life, as a child or adult, to help them to have the courage to build their own careers.

For example, before Britney Spears got her big break, she was truly inspired by Madonna, one of the biggest pop stars of the eighties and still rolling with the times. Madonna, in my opinion, is a legend.

Another great example is the newest addition to country music, Carrie Underwood. As she inspires us, she was inspired by other greats like Rascal Flatts and Shania Twain.

The difference between them and us is once they make it big, they are within that realm of stardom. A devoted fan can sometimes turn into being an equal, or even a companion to the inspiration. Contact between the two is sometimes an everyday affair, whether they are having dinner together, traveling together, working together or just being acquainted with each other. Wouldn't it be cool to wine and dine with Ryan Seacrest? In our wildest dreams and after too much wine is more like it.

Britney Spears at twenty-five had already made herself one of the biggest names in Hollywood. Through the best and the worst, she has managed to keep her head up and stand beside the best of the best. She stirs the pot of controversy while performing with her inspiration, Madonna, at the *Video Music Awards*, and even collaborates with Madonna in her video, "Me Against the Music."

Carrie Underwood began her journey on the hit reality television show *American Idol*, but had already been handed the opportunity of a lifetime when she performed alongside Rascall Flatts before she was even voted the season four winner. Today, she stands beside Brad Paisley hosting the *American Country Music Awards*, introducing great country stars like George Strait, Kenny Chesney and even presenters, such as her personal favorite inspiration, Shania Twain.

Sometimes when you have something that's right within your reach and you get used to it, it is easy to forget what it's like being on the other side of the fence. I am not discrediting celebrities in any way. I know from the fans' perspective that we cannot even begin to understand the pressures of being a star.

I think of some of the downfalls of stardom include the lack of privacy, the breakneck pace of success, dealing with pressures and stress which can sometimes lead to bad decisions, and even loneliness at times. Then, I wonder, why do we all want their lives? Maybe we are the lucky ones.

Britney Spears suffered through more bad publicity than anyone should have to deal with. As I tuned into her documentary "For the Record," I sat and cried with her.

I personally feel that when young teens enter the music industry and become famous pop stars, as they are enjoying the bliss of being a new celebrity, they miss out on the normalcy and the everyday life that every teenager should experience. Then people wonder why they have breakdowns later in life. They are expected to stay on these hectic schedules where they don't even have time to think. Then, one day they come to realize that they need something else in their lives other than the fame, as the same thing one day to the next becomes boring. Even though it starts out exciting and is always fun, they start to crave freedom and, better yet, love the very things we possess and sometimes take for granted. Sometimes I wonder if a person who has what seems to be everything, really has nothing.

As we all make mistakes in our lives or go through times of depression or bad spells, we try to pick up the pieces and move on. In Britney's case, the media made it impossible for her to have any private life at all. They make it impossible for celebrities to pick up the pieces when they have a bad day and instead turn it into a bad week, month or even a year.

After all, if regular people make mistakes, hardly anyone knows about it, but if a celebrity flushes the toilet the wrong way, it's on the front page of *The Enquirer*. I wish Britney the best. I know she will make a comeback sooner than later and I will be nothing but happy for her.

Is it possible to experience the dream and stay grounded, still have a connection to what is reality and avoid all negative influences?

The fan - so many of us which in comparison makes the celebrity scene such a small fraction of the world, yet seen all over the world; and not to forget, who put them where they are.

So, what is my inspiration for writing? The wonder of it all stems from questions derived from three unanswered fan letters.

"Fame is the thirst of youth"
~ Lord Byron

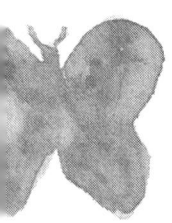

"There is always one moment in childhood when the door opens and lets the future in."
~ Graham Greene

"Happiness lies in the joy of achievement and the thrill of creative effort."
~ Franklin D. Roosevelt

Chapter 2
The Pre-teen/Teenage Fan

My first memory of being a devoted fan was around grade three.

My dad told my mom when I was born, "This one's going to Hollywood." Sorry dad, I'm not there yet, and as the days just keep on passing me by, I'm thinking that I missed the boat on that one.

As a child I loved the camera and the camera loved me. I loved to take part in school plays, even if it was the smallest part, and at home I liked to fool around with the video camera always finding a way to involve my older brother, David, in my silliness.

I remember one time I made him videotape me as a weather forecaster. I dressed up in a yellow rain jacket and pulled up the hood with the string pulled so tight that all you could see was my face. I went out on the front porch in the middle of hurricane Bob and almost got blown right off the steps. We laughed for days as we watched it over and over again.

Being raised in what I considered to be a musical family, I grew up to have a great appreciation for music. My mom played piano and I have memories of hearing her playing the songs "The Entertainer" and "Midnight Fire Alarm" as I was hanging around in my bedroom.

I always wanted to play the piano when I listened to my mom play. I attempted to take lessons twice from two different teachers. Unfortunately, I never had the patience to sit and practice the way I needed in order to succeed. I just wanted to sit and play. I enjoyed sounding things out by ear. Once in a while, I made an attempt to learn a song by actually reading the music. As I always thought it was difficult to read and play at the same time, I would memorize it so that I could just sit and play. I don't think I ever learned a complete song, just bits and pieces of songs, enough to say that I could read music and play a little.

My dad was also in a band. I remember the guys coming over to practice every once in a while. My dad played the drums, John was on the lead guitar, Al on the bass and Andy played the accordion. At my father's annual Super Bowl party, Andy is always there.

Whenever I hear the song "Lyin' Eyes" on the radio, I always think of my dad because I remember him singing that with the band. I also remember "Peaceful Easy Feeling." Hmm, they must have been Eagles fans.

David, my brother, was also a great drummer. In junior high, everyone oohed and ahhed his solo drum performance to "Wipe Out" at the school concerts. I was always proud to be his sister. He has now become more focused on the guitar and is now an incredible guitarist. He is presently working on his own CD, writes his own music and is pretty much a one man band because he can play any instrument.

More than learning how to play an instrument, my heart was set on singing. I have loved to sing since I was about eight years old. I went through a phase where I loved the Broadway musical *Annie*. I made my parents bring me to see the movie in the theater several times.

I had everything "Annie"; the dolls and toys, the clothes and of course the album, which I sang to over and over. I even had this weird idea that I was going to round up the neighborhood kids to perform the production of "Annie" in my backyard. Of course, that never happened.

In fifth grade, I went to Nature's Classroom, an outdoor educational experience, and learned a song that we sang every night around the campfire. I believe it was called "The Garden Song." I loved the song and I really wanted to sing it. I came home with it memorized and sang it to David. "Inch by inch and row by row, gonna make this garden grow, all you need is a rake and a hoe and a piece of fertile ground." He learned it on his guitar by ear and by the end of the night, we had made a tape. We gave it to my mom and dad as a gift and they still have it to this day.

David started to interest me in the Monkees and the Beatles. It was good music and of course, as the little sister who looked up to her big brother, I wanted to do everything that he did and like everything he liked. We performed a lot of Beatles' songs in the basement of our house. Sometimes we fought about who was going to get to sing what songs. I claimed the song "Let It Be," one of my personal favorites.

I remember being really angry with him for not letting me be part of his rendition of "We Are the World." He carried on for five minutes singing the chorus at the end, like it would have killed him to let me sing one lousy verse. Brothers! We did come together to perform for the family on Christmas Eve and even at my cousin Suzie's graduation party, which was mostly just our family and her college friends.

I entered junior high school, joined the chorus and played the recorder, all the usual things that junior high students get involved in. At this time, David and I had a friend, John, who lived about five houses down the street from us. He played the keyboard. We had a goal to make a recording of "Stairway to Heaven." John played the keyboard, David was on the guitar and I actually played the recorder and sang. We had a lot of fun with it and a lot of good laughs, and it sounded pretty good. We only reached the part when the song started to get a little more intense: "and as we wind on down the road…" I never really pictured myself as the rock singer and I will probably never be accused for trying.

In junior high, I aspired to become a cheerleader and was crushed when I didn't make the team. The music teacher, Mrs. C., told me that it was a good thing that I didn't because all of that yelling would have strained my vocal chords and would have ruined my beautiful voice. I actually bought into that, being the dope that I was. It did make me feel better, though.

My best friend, Kiara, and I were fans of all the same musical artists. We were typical pre-teen girls who wore fifty black jelly bracelets, cross earrings, lace ribbons in our hair, lace gloves with the fingertips cut off and denim jackets. We even tried to get away with the midriff shirts which were looked down upon by our parents. We would have sleepovers and spend endless hours dressing up and performing together and solo, making up dances and pretending to sing into fake microphones. Sometimes, I think that we actually thought we were Madonna or that we could be her if we tried hard enough or sang long enough.

We were also huge Michael Jackson fans. My Auntie Becky got a Michael Jackson impersonator for my cousin Marge's birthday one year. She told her that in response to her fan letter she wrote to him, he came to her birthday party. She did not believe it, though. We would have sleepovers and wear the white sequin glove, taking turns to see who could do the moonwalk the best. I think David was always the best at it. It worked easiest with socks on the kitchen floor. I remember shopping for the poster of Michael Jackson in the white suit with the yellow vest. That is the poster everyone had to have and I think all of my friends had it. Another Michael memory was going to my friend Tricia's birthday party to watch the making of *Thriller*. After that, I did not sleep for about a month.

Being a fan as a kid didn't end there.

When my family finally got home from whatever that day had in store, there was the mirror. What kid has not at one point in their lives stood in front of the mirror, performing and singing like we were someone important?

My mother walked into my room once and caught me singing in the mirror to Vanessa Williams', "Save the Best for Last." I was so embarrassed and completely mortified.

Of course, there were also the millions of buttons that we had on our denim jackets, the countless magazines from which we cut out the smallest pictures to add to our own personal homemade wallpaper that covered every inch of paint on the wall and closet doors. I think that double-sided tape was one of the best things that we had in the eighties. Among my personal favorites were Madonna, Michael Jackson, Bon Jovi and of course, Kirk Cameron.

By the end of the sixth grade, I had made a lot of new friends, including my friend Leslie, who I thought was an excellent pianist. We would get together and she would play and I would sing. We gave up before we completed the first verse of "The Greatest Love of All."

Between the unfinished piano music, the half completed version of "Stairway to Heaven," and never getting through "The Greatest Love of All," it sounds like I am a very flighty person, never completing a project. Although I could be seen as a jack of all trades and master of none, I actually am a very thorough and organized person. When I don't complete a project, it drives me crazy. I have sleepless nights walking the floors thinking about all the things that I didn't finish. I will probably never return to those childhood projects but will always use them as a catalyst to set future goals and to accomplish bigger and better things.

It was Leslie that introduced me to what I thought was the best tape ever created, called *Out Of The Blue*. From that point on, I discovered my biggest childhood idol, Debbie Gibson. I was a forever fan and the obsession grew every day. When I encountered my first school dance and was introduced to the "Lip Sync Contest," I knew what I needed to do. I needed to be her.

Two of my friends, Lori and Jan, were willing to be my back up dancers. I spent countless hours in front of the television when I came home from school and after dinner, watching the videos and learning all of the dance moves. I also held several after school sessions with Lori and Jan to teach them all the routines.

As the contest grew closer, I needed a costume. Even though I left this part for the last minute, there it was: the red bandana, the denim jacket, and jeans. These were all pieces that were already a part of my everyday wardrobe.

When the night came, I was so excited. We all got there early so that we could practice in the gym before we were introduced in the cafeteria, which at the time seemed so big. I remember the rush I got when we went on stage. The crowd of teachers and classmates cheered for us and sang along to "Shake Your Love." We ended up winning second place. The prize was twenty dollars and after splitting it three ways, we all brought home six dollars and fifty cents each. It didn't matter because we were all so proud of ourselves.

The following year, my friend Melanie and I joined the same lip sync contest, this time performing "Out Of The Blue." Costumes consisted of black hats and high-waist plaid miniskirts; again, items of clothing pulled straight from the everyday wardrobe. We didn't win that year but still had a blast.

My obsession lasted throughout junior high and most of high school.

I remember having my first boyfriend, Darren, when I was a sophomore, and writing love letters and notes quoting the lyrics from her songs. Thinking that there is a slim possibility that he may still have those is kind of scary to me. In saying that, I don't think guys keep that kind of crap that all of we girls do.

I did, however, manage to get to two of her concerts.

My cousins Marge and Cielia brought me and my two friends, Kiara and Irene, to the first concert. My cousins were utterly embarrassed by us because we were all dressed up. We, at the time, thought we were cat's asses but looking back, just asses would probably be a more appropriate description. We had floor seats and could not see a thing, but just the thrill of being there was great.

I went to the second concert with my cousin Tori and we had really good seats. I was a little older and I remember dancing with her through most of the show and having the best time. I actually still have the program from that show. I even remember having to buy these earrings that she was wearing on the cover of the program which were these silver stick figures of a boy and a girl.

Taping the videos on *MTV* was my favorite pastime. I remember waiting for hours for them to come on and then got so excited when they finally did. I would then watch the tapes over and over, forward and rewind, until I knew them well enough to perform on my own to the music.

I desperately wanted to join the annual lip sync contest in high school and to perform "Electric Youth." I gathered my friends Tori, Kami and Ava, but we could never quite get it together to perform. Back in the day, that's what being a fan was all about. It was all innocent and all in good fun.

Today, my cousin Cielia remembers the embarrassment I caused her the night of my first concert. As she laughs, so do I because now having an eight year old daughter of her own, my Debbie Gibson is her daughter's Hannah Montana.

For all kids, their idols are inspirations to a promising future, whether it is to follow in their footsteps or go to college and start a different career. No matter what they decide, those admirations and memories are always with them and will follow them throughout their lives in some way, shape, or form. For some, it is just a childhood dream but to others, a sought after reality. Whatever the outcome, childhood idols have a great influence on their young fans somewhere throughout their lives. Hopefully, it is a positive, lasting impression.

For me, well, I still wear jelly bracelets and high-waist puffy skirts. Just kidding... but don't laugh, there is a good chance that we will be wearing that stuff again real soon, as we are still revisiting the bell bottoms and tie-dye t-shirts of the seventies.

Growing Up

1977 — Mom, Dave and Me
Connecticut

1981 — First Grade Play
A piece of lettuce in
Peter Rabbit's Garden

1981 — Dave and me practicing
in basement

1982 — Piano Recital

1986 — Junior High Play "Ashpet" [Taken from The Landmark]

Debbie Gibson Days

1989 — Dave and Me After Disney

1993 — Dave and Me Spirit of Boston Cruise

1993 — Christmas Eve Dad, Dave and me

"You may only be someone in the world, but to someone else, you may be the world."
~ Unknown

"A celebrity is a person who works hard all his life to become well known, then wears dark glasses to avoid being recognized."
~ Fred Allen

Chapter 3
The Fan

Although the star or celebrity gets to live the souped up lifestyle in the Hollywood hills, the fan is the one who is responsible for getting them there. If one of them were to make a movie and nobody was interested in seeing it, or if one of them recorded an album and nobody bought it, where would they be? Without the fan, there is no star.

I am a fan of many actors, actresses and musical artists. As a devoted fan, I look at every one of them as an individual. Although the movie and music star both have their share of obsessive fans, in my opinion, I feel that they also have very different fan bases.

A movie star like Brad Pitt or Julia Roberts is much harder to come by. I feel that they are more stationary and the chances of meeting one of them is slim to none, unless you live in Los Angeles or New York, which are still two very big places. I do know of some fans that were lucky enough to be in the same area when they were filming a movie and got to sneak a peak, which could definitely be a very exciting experience. Most of our exchanges with them involve watching them on the big screen, where you don't get to know the actual actor, Tom Cruise, but instead as the character of Maverick or Jerry Maguire, "Show me the money!"

Our relationship with television celebrities is the same. Do we really know Jennifer Aniston? The answer is no. We knew and loved her in the role of Rachel Greene, one of our best *Friends*. We do get to know a little about these big stars on talk shows but as every one knows, a five minute segment is not a lot of time to really get to know a person.

Last of all is the media, magazines and tabloids, and one never knows if what is printed is ever really the truth. Of course, we all buy them and read them because we love a little good gossip every now and then. Let's face it; we will never get to know even a small piece of who these people really are any more than they will ever know us.

The recording artist, in my opinion, is quite different. Many musical artists tour around the world. Some of them are actually more accessible to their fans and sometimes on a more personal level. They are also not playing the role of anyone but themselves. What you see is what you get. Going to a concert for a fan is a moving experience. Just being in the same vicinity as someone you are a die hard fan of, whether the seats are the best in the house or the worst, produces a rush I am sure that most people have experienced.

Personality definitely comes out through song and dance and many fans can relate to lyrics in songs that are sung by their favorite artists. I have always believed that music is what feelings sound like. Most artists who take the stage at a concert will talk to their fans and occasionally even bring them up on stage to be part of the show. There are also backstage passes or meet and greets, where fans can hang out with the stars of the show, get autographs, pictures and other memorabilia.

These types of exchanges between a fan and a celebrity make a fan feel important, but sometimes also very vulnerable. This is because they allow us to get closer to them, like an invitation to come up on stage or at a meet and greet. When you get the chance to get that close to someone who on a daily basis seems untouchable, it gives us hope that they will somehow let us into their world in some way or another.

I guess maybe it is a good thing that I have never been the recipient of backstage passes or lucky enough to attend a meet and greet. I would definitely think that, hey, if I can get this close to Justin Timberlake, maybe I can ask him to go out for a cup of coffee. I certainly would not do that, but undeniably, we would all like to think it's a possibility.

Although I am a fan of a lot of actors and actresses, on a more personal note, I seem to be more taken with musical artists. I have not been to many concerts, probably less than fifteen, which is a lot to some and so little to others. They have all been very different experiences. This is because there are also different types of fans. As fans, we also like to be looked at as individuals. I am a different type of fan to each artist that I admire. In speaking about these different types of fans, we can all probably put ourselves into one or more of the following categories. I have encountered each type of fan at every show that I have ever attended.

Let's start with *The Confused Fan*. As a fan of the band or artist that we are fond of because we heard one of their songs on the radio that we liked, we will buy the whole CD for just one song if the single is not available. After buying it, we realize that the other tracks are just okay, and then after burning the song we originally liked onto a mix CD, it gets shelved.

Now that we are living in the millennium, we may not even buy the whole CD but download the one song from iTunes, the artist still making a profit. It turns out that we are actually more a fan of the song than the actual artist.

I can easily recall some of the CD's that I bought that fit this category while I was growing up. Now come on, you can admit it; everyone has rocked out to the great "Tubthumper" by Chumba Wumba, sung along like a child to the addictive "Mmm Bop" by Hanson, or has strut their stuff to one of my personal favorites, "I'm Too Sexy" by Right Said Fred. The list goes on but we must not forget the unforgettable, everybody say it now, "Whooomp, There It Is."

Then, there is the *Run of the Mill* Fan. This type of fan will buy the CD and love almost every song on it. We consider them a favorite artist and in time, we will probably own all of their releases, including the greatest hits CD, which usually includes all of the stuff we already own. The recordings of this artist then get the privilege of being kept in the CD holder in the car because it is listened to on a regular basis. When tickets go on sale, we are definitely going to be there to see this artist live in concert. We will gather friends and family who are also interested in this artist and will go to the show to have an exciting night out.

I would say that most of the shows I have been to fit into this category. Some of my personal favorites are Madonna, Mariah Carey, No Doubt, Gwen Stefani, Bon Jovi, Aerosmith and the Cranberries.

I remember going to see the Cranberries at the Boston Pavilion, now the Bank of America Pavilion, with my husband, Bryce, and brother. We had the worst seats ever but it did not matter because we were there. It was freezing cold and anyone who knows the Pavilion knows that it is an outdoor show. We were all bundled up in layers but we had the best time listening to the music, singing along and dancing to try to keep warm. On the way home, we were still excited. We talked about the show, how great it was and how we all had the best time. It evolves into an unforgettable night as we return home, hoping for a new CD and the chance to see them again.

The confused fan and the run of the mill fan are every star's dream. We purchase their CDs and sometimes attend their shows when they are coming to our area. We enjoy the music and performances and they plug their upcoming CD because they know we are going to buy it, no strings attached, end of story. The truth is that it doesn't always stop there.

The Obsessive Fan usually has a favorite artist, one unlike any other, one in which they are extremely focused upon. Most likely, this fan feels some kind of a connection with the artist. This is the CD that we can hardly wait to be released, and after we rush to the store to buy it, it stays in the CD player for more days than not. It follows us into the house and back into the car because we can't stand to be without it.

Every song is memorized and looking forward to a concert becomes a part of our everyday life. We tune into talk shows to see what is going on in our idols' lives. We buy any magazine or book that splashes our idols picture on the cover. We may write an occasional fan letter in hope to connect with our idol with that one percent chance that we may get a response. No, we are not crazy, but we want to believe that our letter is special.

We are usually grounded but for some reason seem to need the extra excitement in our life. We want to believe that we are on the same wavelength as our idol and we think of ourselves as more of a friend than a fan. More times than not, there is an attraction to our idol in more ways than one. We are attracted to the piece of them that is a musical artist, attracted to their personality and/or sense of humor and most likely attracted to them physically.

In my experience, there have been two times in my life in the past seven years that fit into this category. My experience as an obsessive fan has been both a fun and frustrating adventure for me, somehow developing into somewhat of an unsolved mystery. If you fit into this category, you may be able to relate to my experience, which I like to refer to as, my *American Idol* experience.

If you are a little crazier than the obsessive fan, then you are probably the *Irrational Obsessive Fan*. This is the fan who as a teenager or an adult spends three quarters of their time online reading about their idol or arguing on an unofficial website with other fans about who is going to meet their idol first and which one has the better chance of a marriage proposal. Not only do you buy tickets to a show in your area, but buy tickets to several shows or to every show on the tour to watch the same show over again. You may become known as a "groupie." When you show up for the show, you could possibly have the front row seats or backstage passes and could have possibly paid thousands of dollars for them from a ticket broker or from eBay. You consider this an opportunity to touch, get close to or possibly meet your idol. You might adopt a new style or maybe keep your everyday look of dressing head to toe from hats and t-shirts to handbags and earrings with your idol's face on it. These items may even be homemade. You may carry signs that read, "Will you marry me?" or "Can I hug you?" These signs can be creative and quite humorous to others, but because you made them and hold them up high for your idols to see during the show, you take them seriously.

I always want to be inside of a celebrity's head when they see this type of fan because I would love to know what he or she is thinking. I always wonder if he enjoys this or does it make him uneasy? I have never been one to wear a concert t-shirt to a show. I guess I feel that if I ever got a chance to meet my idol, I would want to look at him as a down to earth person and I would want him to look at me the same way without feeling uneasy.

It is almost guaranteed that at least one of these types of fans becomes a stars worst nightmare...*The Stalker*.

Beware, *The Stalker.* I don't know much about this type of fan because I have never seen or encountered one in any of my experiences. I would say that the stalker is the fan gone mad.

The unfortunate thing is that they don't think that they are a stalker. Most of them don't even mean any harm but as they "create their own reality" and then are rejected they can become angry and sometimes violent.

There are many celebrities who have unfortunately experienced the stalker such as Uma Thurman, Debbie Gibson, Jeff Goldblum, Michael Douglas, Cheryl Crow, Gwyneth Paltrow, Mel Gibson and Anna Kournikova.

Although most of the time issuing a restraining order does the trick, some stalkers are actually convicted.

I can definitely understand why celebrities would fear this type of fan. Celebrities can never be too careful because you just never know. There are a lot of crazies out there and it is this type of fan that ruins it for the rest of us. In truth though, we are not all crazies.

"I handle fame by not being famous.
I am not famous to me."
~ Bob Marley

"Fame and Tranquility can never be bedfellows."
~ Michel de Montaigne

"Rather than love, than money, than fame,
give me truth."
~ Henry David Thoreau

Chapter 4
The Separation of the Universes

Is there a fine line between celebrities and their fans? Where exactly do celebrities stand with their fans? How much of themselves are they willing to give us? What can we expect from them? Why can't we talk to them? Will we ever know the answers to these questions? Probably not, but we can explore the possible answers. Where we stand with our famed favorites is a much different story than where they stand with us, or is it?

It is true that some of us just want in on the "bling." Although I cannot speak for our celebrities, I think it would be a fair guess to say that it is difficult for them because after they reach celebrity status, it is hard to know if someone is just interested in them for their money. In today's world, you never know. I am sure there are many men and women out there that just want to marry a star so that they can be well off for the rest of their lives, live life in the fast lane and get lots of publicity by being in the limelight. Although being pampered and spoiled is sometimes nice, money is not everything. Although having money can make life easier, it is definitely not the most important thing and it does not buy happiness. The Beatles had it right when they sang, "Can't Buy Me Love."

Personally, for me, it is not about the money. I would never want to be rich, just comfortable. I really believe that having too much has a negative effect on people. I would never want a home with more rooms than I could use or a car that costs more than a college education. I would not change one thing about my lifestyle. The most important thing is just to be happy. I actually enjoy giving much more than getting. However, I would love to have my own recording studio to fulfill my passion for singing and music. Oh, and of course I would love my own physical trainer so that I could look like Britney Spears in her *MTV Video Music Awards* performance in the year 2000. Most of all, I will never give up the fantasy of having some kind of relationship with my idol, but how close is too close?

Not receiving a response to my letters bothered me more and more, and so I had an interesting conversation with my friend, Elizabeth, which started me thinking even more.

For the last few years, she had actually had an interesting relationship with someone in the music industry. It all started when she was online inquiring about her idol and came across an icon that said "Say hi." Curious, she clicked on it and simply left a message that read, "Thank you for all the great music." To her surprise, she actually got a response. From that point on, they were quite friendly. She had several conversations with him on email and in person while attending several of his shows. One day, she asked him to have a cup of coffee with her and he immediately put up a wall. It was as if the emails and personal conversations were fine, but once she took it a step further, it was an absolute no-no. Is there a law against having a cup of coffee with a fan or is that just too personal? Do celebrities fear getting too close to a fan?

If there is chemistry or even the grounds for a solid friendship, why is this so wrong? What is crossing the line?

Anyway, Elizabeth told me to be happy that I never got a response to my letters and that things would be better off that way. She said that for whatever reason, they do not want to get personal with us and that we should not try to get personal with them. This was because through her experience, becoming close had led to nothing but her feeling crushed.

I remember our Aunt Carol and Uncle Tony taking Bryce and I on what was my first and only trip to New York City. I was so excited to visit the Big Apple. New York City is definitely the place where no one sleeps at night.

It has always been my dream to visit both New York City and California because both are affiliated with the stars. As I still await that trip to California, I was going to enjoy New York to its fullest.

In one night and two days, we toured most of the city. We even went on a horse and carriage ride through Central Park. It was really fun but I kept giggling on and off throughout most of the ride because for some reason all I could think of was that episode of *Seinfeld* when Kramer kept feeding the horse the baked beans. Yes, it is true, we live in a world where farts are funny and the farting horse to me was even funnier. I cannot understand people who do not find humor in comedians like Jim Carrey and Steve Carrell. It is important to be able to laugh at the simple things in life.

We also went to see *Beauty and the Beast* on Broadway. As I dressed up that night all in black wearing a hat, I felt like a movie star. I walked the streets of New York City and looked around just hoping to see one celebrity. Uncle Tony told me that I had probably walked by several of them but never would have known it because in reality, they are just like me. In truth, the thread that they used to make those $2,000 jeans is no different than the thread they used to make mine, Old Navy style.

I am assuming that the biggest issue is the difference in class and also living completely different lifestyles in almost completely different worlds. When do you ever see a celebrity befriend, date or marry someone other than another celebrity? It rarely, if ever, occurs. This is because it is so much easier to be with someone who naturally lives the same lifestyle, dare we blend the two.

Succumbing to some type of realism, no matter how hard it may be, we fans do have to take some accountability for the way we perceive the separation of the two universes. If we were to befriend or capture the heart of our most admired idol, would we actually be able to deal with and accept their way of life? We are not at all accustomed to that type of lifestyle; always on the road, missing out on quality time, never seeing some who are most important in life, giving up privacy and freedom, leaving behind family and friends, and perhaps even loneliness. Again, is it really the dream?

If I wasn't married and got a chance to meet my idol and had an opportunity to have a romantic relationship with him, I'm not sure

I could handle it. I would want his undivided attention all of the time and would not take it lightly when he would have to leave me behind, especially if there were children involved. The difficulty in never knowing what is really going on or not playing an active role in what we are accustomed to as the family life makes me wonder, would it ever last?

I have observed through magazines and entertainment news shows that many stars are either not married or have been married several times. If it is impossible to make a marriage work with someone within their own status, how can we be hopeful about the success in uniting two people of completely different worlds? Sometimes I think we want to be affiliated in some way with a star because we are somehow filling a void. In trying to fill that piece of something in our lives that seems to be missing, we try to live our dreams through their reality.

From another point of view, as we would like to live our dreams through their reality, could it be possible that maybe they would like to live their "old lives" through our reality, something they used to have that they occasionally miss?

I continue to go back and forth about the whole fame thing. If I could ask a Hollywood star one question it would be, "which life is better, your old one or your new one?" Sometimes I think that everyone would just like to have their one week of fame and then go back to business as usual. I know that is just another dream, but I think that in truth, it is only the curiosity of the celebrity lifestyle that is so inviting to most people.

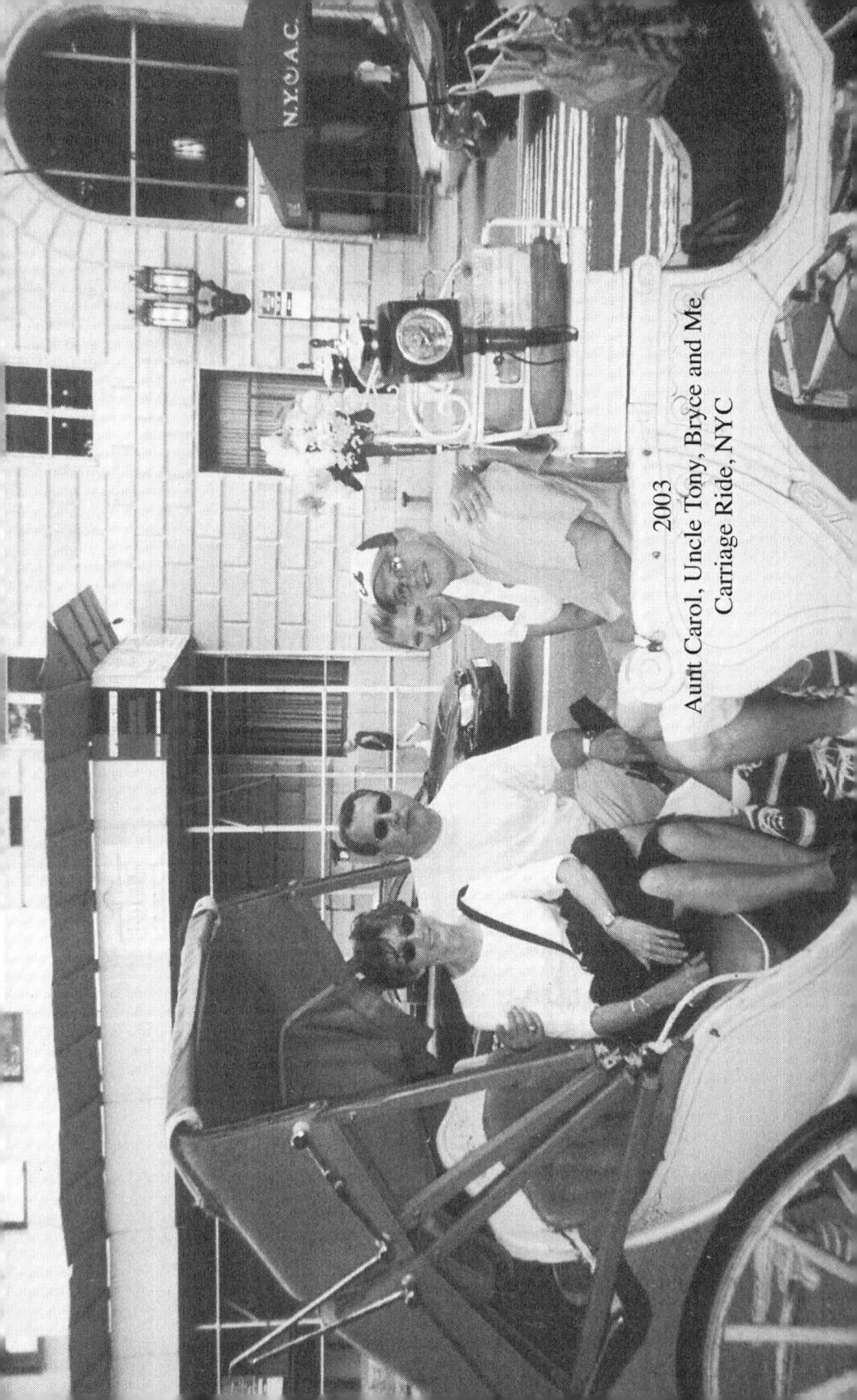

2003
Aunt Carol, Uncle Tony, Bryce and Me
Carriage Ride, NYC

Uncle Tony, Aunt Carol,
Bryce & Me — Times Square

Bryce & Me — NBC Studios

Uncle Tony, Aunt Carol, Bryce & Me —
Home from the Big Apple

"Never take life too seriously.
Nobody gets out alive anyway."
~ Unknown

"The mark of a true crush is that you fall in love first
and grope for reasons afterward."
~ Shana Alexander

Chapter 5
My Idol

What is an idol? One definition explains it as, "One that is adored, often blindly and excessively."

My definition of an idol is not only someone that you adore blindly and excessively but someone you adore for one or more admired qualities, with whom you feel a connection with because of commonalities such as interests, morals and values. Although it is said that opposites attract, I think it is important to have someone in your life with whom you can relate.

I remember in college having a small crush on actor Andrew Shue. As most people were watching *Beverly Hills 90210*, I was a *Melrose Place* junkie. Sometimes when I watch *Desperate Housewives*, I get flashbacks of *Melrose Place*. I still think of Bree Hodge as Kimberly and Tom Scavo as Matt.

I also had a short lived crush on Leonardo DiCaprio after *Romeo and Juliet* came out. The *Titanic* was just another whole phenomenon leading to a pink and silver angel fish named Jack and Rose. I'll give you one guess as to who went belly up first.

I really have not had an idol since junior high school and wondered if it was even normal or healthy to have one at age twenty-eight. At first I kept my feelings very quiet because I was afraid that everyone would think I was crazy. I am definitely a kid at heart and feel that you are never too old for anything. After all, life would be pretty boring if we didn't have that inner child.

Maria, my best friend, was someone I felt I could talk to about anything. We met in college and lived across the hall from each other in our senior year. We always had a lot in common besides the fact that we were the same height, wore the same size and we were both blonde. We had our ups and our downs, but we always had each other's back. We had lost a few years between college graduation and marriage, along with the birth of her first child, due to a falling out. I always regretted letting anything come in between the friendship and I wrote her a letter apologizing. As we started to get together again, things soon got back to where they were. We enjoyed karaoke, never in a public place, and loved reminiscing about the college days when pouring as much salt as we could on the others food without getting caught until the other took a bite was hysterical.

I started to confide in Maria about the secret love affair that was going on only inside my mind revolving around a celebrity obsession. She was the one who convinced me that I was not crazy.

Although it has taken me years, I feel as if I can talk about my ongoing experience as a fan, including some of the crazy thoughts and feelings that led me to do some crazy things.

It all started in January of 2003 when I found myself getting lost in the reality show, *American Idol.* I never watched season one but I was a fan of the winner, Kelly Clarkson. I always heard people talking about season one, especially Maria.

As I have always had a passion for singing, I thought I would tune in to season two of *American Idol*. I watched the show week after week and grew from liking it to loving it, and then to loving him.

From the first time I laid eyes on him, I was intrigued. As I liked many of the top twelve contestants, for some reason I was really drawn to him. I looked forward to his particular performance every week and found myself getting excited when it was his turn to perform. My strong liking grew into what I would consider a small crush.

I had assumed the role of junior high guidance counselor at a small school in Massachusetts for four years. Previously, I had worked with special education students for two years. Knowing that my idol had a similar experience in the work field before he rose to stardom, I felt that we automatically shared something in common.

I had built a lot of great relationships with most of my students and a few selective co-workers. Therefore, it was not unusual for me to come into work in the morning and have a picture of my obsession on my office door or the most recent *People* magazine sitting on my desk.

I even had one student come into my office after a doctor's appointment and hand me a picture that she had torn out of one of the magazines in the waiting area at the doctor's office. After I told her that I had appreciated that she was thinking of me and that I knew she meant well, I had to explain to her why it was wrong for her to tear the picture out of a magazine that was not hers. After she left my office, I smiled and laughed to myself.

Although some people despise the junior high age, the middle school student, in my opinion, is the best. This is because they are always making me laugh even when they are not trying to be funny.

As I sat back down at my desk, I felt that I was being watched from every direction with all of the pictures collected from students. As a guidance counselor, it was my main priority to be there for the kids but in a lot of ways, they were also there for me. These kids kept me going and kept the excitement alive in my life. As a twenty-eight year old, more times than not I was mistaken for a student.

When I was a junior high and high school student, I was not the most popular girl in the class. I did not fit into cliques well because I felt I should be able to be friends with who I want, date who I want and not be judged for it. I was also the good girl and there were times when my own friends did not want to take "mom" to the party. I paid for this my first three years of high school. You would think things would be different in a Catholic school but when I changed schools two weeks into my senior year, it ended up being one of the best years of my life.

I felt that I did my job as a counselor well because my students saw me as a cool friend rather than a teacher or counselor. When the junior high students came to visit me in my office, it was because they looked up to me and my advice was important to them. I felt that I got through to a lot of them because I didn't look the part of mom, but I still preached the part of mom.

When the high school boys dropped in to visit, it was not for advice but just to flirt. I even had one student ask me out. As I looked at him in disbelief, he told me he would get a note from his mother. As it made me feel young at heart, this was the one time I felt it may be better to look the part of mom. Bryce always joked about the students having crushes on me and would start to sing that David Lee Roth song, "Hot for Teacher." I would get all uptight because it just made me uncomfortable.

Throughout my obsession with music, movies, celebrities and *American Idol*, there was one time in the school year that allowed me to indulge in the roots of what I thoroughly enjoyed. In April, on the last day of Spirit Week, was the annual lip sync contest. Not only did I help the kids create an *American Idol* performance, but I also coordinated the faculty production two years in a row. The first year was a compilation of music through the decades. I not only got to play Madonna by performing "Material Girl," but also made a cute Baby Spice performing "Wanna Be" with four other members of the faculty as, none other than, the Spice Girls.

The second year, I moved to movies. I played Foxy Cleopatra with Austin Powers, and Garth from *Wayne's World*, singing "Bohemian Rhapsody." The kids loved it both years. They love to see it when you actually take a step back from the role of teacher/counselor and reach them at a different level of craziness.

As the month of May grew closer, the finale of *American Idol* neared. I watched the last show and called in to place my vote like every other week. Unfortunately, I was not able to watch the final show live on results night.

Bryce and I had tickets to a Red Sox game on the same night. I remember having to tape it and would not let him listen to the radio on the way home because I did not want to know who won until I could go home and watch it. This, of course, was a tape that I should have burned rather than watched. This is because what I had waited all night to be excited about turned into total disappointment. I reacted to it with such anger as my husband laughed at me with disbelief. My anger then turned to tears. I had sworn I would never watch the show again, which obviously, I quickly got over.

I think that we all act as if it were we that lost a major competition when that dedicated to a particular artist. We act so ridiculously. I mean, really, it is not like anybody died or lost a limb or something, so is there any excuse for us to act like this at all? Probably not, but we do.

I had a hard time getting to work the morning after. This was because not only was I exhausted from being in Boston for a Sox game and then coming home to watch a two hour tape, but I was also royally pissed off.

I sat in my office that morning and I thought, "How crazy would it be for me to write a fan letter?" This is something that I had never done, and probably under most circumstances would never do. I always thought that writing a fan letter was silly. Do we really know where it is that they actually go? Does it ever really reach them? Do they really read it, if it does reach them? If it does reach them, do they really read it or does someone else read it for them, which to me would be a total waste of my time? I went online wondering, "What are the chances of the address being other than the Los Angeles one where all of the fans send their mail?" I thought that maybe because he is not that big yet, it would be possible that I could find another address where he would maybe actually receive it. Then, I found an address that looked like it might be worth a try, so I figured, "What the hell?" and began typing.

Dear Idol,

This is the first time that I have ever written a fan letter in my life. What are the odds of you personally reading this letter? I guess we will see since I am not even sure that I have the correct address.

I am twenty eight years old and a guidance counselor in a small town in Massachusetts. I live in Worcester and I am extremely excited about the show at the Worcester Centrum on July 25th, my birthday. It is probably the best birthday present I could ever have.

I will admit that I was disappointed in the results of American Idol, *Season 2, but every time one of my students comes into my office angry about it, I need to explain to them that despite the number of votes, you were truly a winner and that you will be huge, or should I say, you already are. You definitely have the most outstanding voice that I have ever heard and I cannot wait until your CD is released.*

Most importantly, unlike most crazed fans, I don't know a whole lot about you, but after watching you from week to week, I know that you are a wonderful person on the inside and that is what really matters. I admire that you work with children to make a difference in their lives.

You are naturally goodhearted and you seem to have a wonderful set of values. You are truly an inspiration and a positive influence to society. You are caring, sensitive and extremely classy and the definition of what a true idol is. You ARE "the whole package" and guys like you are one in a million.

Congratulations on your success and good luck in the future. Whatever you decide to do in life at this point, remember to follow your dreams and don't let anyone bring you down. If I had only one wish, besides world peace and to hang out with you for a day, it would be to have met you before you were untouchable. Don't ever let money and fame change the wonderful person you are.

After the letter was completed, I put it into an envelope with my school's return address on it and thought, *If he sees that it is coming from a school will it be more important? Would he come to perform here, at a school, where he has so many admirers, including myself? How cool would that be?* Am I a dreamer or what? Who cares? The dream lives.

I mailed it that afternoon from the town post office the next street over. I even went as far as to joke with the postman about it being very important and as he looked at it he chuckled. I definitely joked with him as a cover because I was so embarrassed about what I was doing. I was a twenty-eight year old married woman sending a fan letter to a twenty-four year old who had no idea who I was and probably did not care. I did not even mention being married in the letter. Then, the waiting and waiting and more waiting began. Would I get a response? I think the worst feeling in the world for a fan is the anticipation.

Finally, a time comes when all the hype wears down and you are faced with the big reality slap that it's not going to happen. I wondered what I was thinking and if I was a complete idiot, or have I lost my mind? After getting my head out of the clouds and coming somewhat back down to Earth, I concluded that the letter had never reached him and someone else must have had a good laugh on me. At least, this is what I wanted to think.

"Success is the ability to go from one failure to another with no loss of enthusiasm."
~ Winston Churchill

"Never give up on something you can't stop thinking about."
~ Unknown

"Don't be discouraged.
It's often the last key in the bunch that opens the lock."
~ Unknown

Chapter 6
Life Goes On

It is July 25th, 2003, my twenty-ninth birthday, and "This is the Night!" I have never been so excited! We arrived at the Worcester Centrum early so that we could get our programs and find our seats. Our seats were located center stage but they were pretty far back. We had a good view but you definitely needed binoculars to see detail. Luckily, I had borrowed some from my cousin, Marge. I was feeling a lot of anxiety from the anticipation and excitement. As the show began, they started off with the first idol to leave the show and worked their way up. I remember Bryce turning to me and saying, "You have a long wait." In a way, it was good because I had something to anticipate. After the idols all had a chance to perform, they finished the show with a bunch of group performances.

I enjoyed the show, some parts more than others, and I did not want the night to end. Of course, at this point, there wasn't any talk of any future touring so I knew that this may be the last of the excitement for me.

I remember after the show, our group of five, myself, Bryce, David and two of our friends, Jude and Sierra, going to Pub 99 for some buffalo wings and fries. We all had a great time.

As I went to bed that night with a smile on my face, I reflected on the show, about how it was the best birthday ever along with some other thoughts which are better left untold. Suddenly, I found myself being really depressed and sad. I couldn't figure out if it was because a night I had so looked forward to for so long had come and gone so fast or, even crazier, if I was disappointed about some unrealistic dream I had about him possibly acknowledging my birthday, which of course he didn't. I had this deranged expectation of him getting my letter and knowing that I was going to be there on my birthday.

The fact that he receives hundreds of letters a day had no effect on my hope that this was not in a million years going to happen. Actually, it did, but that is not something that any fan wants to accept. I did have something to look forward to, a CD that would be released in October.

Come October, I was counting down the days. I remember the day really well. I was about eight weeks pregnant. I had actually called in sick to work the day of the release so that I could be the first one into Best Buy at ten o'clock a.m. to get the CD. I remember not feeling so good when I got there, so I went into the store and purchased the CD as quickly as I could and rushed back to the car. As I got into the driver's seat, excited to take it out of the wrapper, I noticed there was a huge crack in the front of the CD. I must not have noticed it due to the fact that I was not feeling that great and was trying to get in and out of there in a hurry. I was so pissed off and sat for a minute, questioning whether I should go back and exchange it. In most circumstances, I think I would have lived with the crack, but not this time.

I ran back into the store and got a new one and then rushed back into the car, anxious to hear it. Not feeling well at all, I had to struggle with the wrapper. This is the packaging we all hate when we buy a new CD because it is going to take at least ten minutes to open it.

I was able to listen to some of it on the way home and when I got home, I had my first bout of morning sickness. I kept wondering if God was punishing me for calling in sick to work or if my unborn child did not have the same taste in music as his mother. Come to think of it, I think it was one of the only CDs I listened to throughout my pregnancy and I puked for seven months straight.

At this time, there was talk of my idol touring with first season winner, Kelly Clarkson. I purchased two tickets and on March 8th found myself back at the Worcester Centrum, this time with my mom. I was feeling alright and hoping that my baby would cooperate, which he did. Maybe he had a change of heart. It is said that if a baby hears music in the womb that they recognize it after birth. I do think that he must have because up until this day, he either falls asleep to it every time we take a ride in the car or asks to hear it as he bee bops in the back seat with most of the words memorized.

Again, the show was great. I remember getting this rush when he came on stage through an entrance right through the middle of his fans. I thought it was awesome and quite brave. This time he was the first to perform. The entire time Kelly was performing, all I could think about was whether or not he was coming back. If I could have answered that question with a no, I think I may have gone home.

My mom and I did stay for the remainder of the show. At home, I was excited because I had bought my first t-shirt and couldn't wait to wear it. This time, I was only depressed because I bought my t-shirt in my actual size, an extra small, and I was not by any means tiny. I hoped for another show in the future, which of course, happened.

On August 3, 2004, Bryce drove us to the Ryan Center at the University of Rhode Island. We had no clue where we were going, but it was the closest show to us. We had directions from Jude and Sierra because they had family that owns a summer home nearby.

We ended up getting there an hour early. We had not eaten and did not know the area. With a lot of time to spare, we waited outside amongst the other fans. This is when I really started to take notice of all the different types of fans that were out there.

As I looked around, there were teenage fans running around everywhere. I remember one girl being so out of control it was like entertainment for all of us. There were two girls that caught my eye that were wearing homemade t-shirts that said 'Mrs. ____.' I thought to myself, You've got to be kidding me. I then wondered if that was something that I may have done as a teenager. Well, maybe it's not so crazy. After all, the way that Hollywood and life works today, a ten to twenty year age difference is quite normal. I also began to think, hell, even at an older age, married or single, we actually think quite often of the possibility that our admired idols could somehow be our boyfriends. We at times refer to them as our boyfriends, so who are we kidding here?

There were guys and girls and women and men of all ages, sizes and shapes. It was very interesting what a wide range of fans were actually there. I noticed two people who were directly involved with the artist in the crowd which was very unusual, but I thought it was quite nice. One of them was one of his background singers and he was signing autographs.

The other was his bodyguard, out in the open, listening to people sing and picking out who he thought was best to perform on stage. Even though I had been dying to get the chance to get close to my idol and to fulfill my dream of singing on stage, I do not think that I could handle a situation like that. It is hard to actually know what exactly your reaction would be when it came right down to it and there you are, standing right next to someone you have all of these unexplained crazy feelings for and then being expected to sing, and in front of thousands of people. That is something that I could never do. Even though back in the day I was a "ham for the cam," I found that I had somewhere along the way become very camera shy and developed stage fright. I sometimes like to blame it on the cheerleading incident, my first real form of rejection that I never really overcame.

As soon as we got inside, Bryce got something for us to eat while I waited in the souvenir line. It was my goal to get a good poster or picture because other than being at a show, pictures seemed very hard to come by.

I actually had bid on a picture three times on eBay and don't remember how much I spent on it because at the time I didn't care.

I also brought my own digital camera thinking I could take some of my own pictures.

We found our seats and they were probably the best seats that I had ever had at a concert. It was the best show yet, my third concert, but the first where the stage was all his. The opening act was Cherie, who I had never heard of but I thought to be quite good. I did end up buying her CD. I also envied her to be touring with my idol and thought that if I were in her shoes I would be all over that.

It was at this concert that I found out that he had started a new foundation created to help children with disabilities. Well, now, how did I know that he would do that? It was just another thing that made me admire him a little more, which I did not think was possible.

I took pictures during most of the show. He changed his outfit several times. He started with the basic blue button down with a tie and jeans. During the middle of the show, he had a striped coat with a white t-shirt and jeans. At some point toward the end of the show, he was actually sporting a full white suit. The picture taking in some respects was good and bad. Good, because I got some great shots but bad because I felt that I did not enjoy the show to its fullest because I was so focused on getting good pictures. Therefore, the show seemed to end so fast.

On the way home, I still had adrenaline rushing through my veins. I crawled into bed, still excited, but I started to feel depressed again. At this point in his career, I knew that there was going to be another show so I was not sure from where the sadness was coming.

It lasted for about a week and then all was fine again. I never thought back on it other than to stare at my program every once and a while and to look forward to another show.

I was excited to find out about a Christmas album that would be released. Naturally, I bought it the day it hit the store shelves and listened to it throughout the holidays. I really enjoyed this CD because I really love Christmas music. I was sad to have to stop listening to it come January. It could have been Christmas all year.

I bought two tickets for the Christmas concert for December 3, 2004, at the Providence Performing Arts Center. In November, Bryce blew out his knee playing football with the guys. He had his surgery at the end of November with the concert about two weeks away.

I called the Performing Arts Center to let them know that he was temporarily handicapped and to see if they could make any accommodations for us. I was excited to find out that they would give us handicapped seating and that we could still go.

That night, I drove to the Providence Performing Arts Center. This was quite the experience because anybody who knows me also knows that my biggest fear is driving on big highways or unfamiliar roads. I have this terrible anxiety about getting lost or somehow ending up going the wrong way on a huge highway. There have been times when Bryce has said to me, "What do you think is going to happen? Do you think that the road is just going to end and you are going to fall off into thin air?" I never answer that question because I know if I say yes, I will get laughed at. I have actually seen movies like that where there

71

is a chase and the road just ends and I start screaming because it scares the crap out of me, worse than a horror movie. Anyway, despite being nervous, I was determined to get to the show.

As I drove down route 146, palms sweating, I was doing fine until we ran into route 95, a five lane highway with a butt load of cars. I thought I was going to get the two of us killed but luckily God was with me because it was the first exit, after merging into the madness, we needed to take.

When we got there, we found parking and Bryce crutched his way to the theater. The ushers were kind enough to meet us at the door and wheel him into our seats, which were in the very front of the theater. These seats were even better than the last show. This was one of the only benefits to my husband's unfortunate situation.

The one thing that stunk was I got my camera taken from me before we entered the theater. I was not worried about the camera being safe but we were so close that I could have really taken some sweet pictures.

I went to buy us some food, my program and some souvenirs. Bryce had to keep his leg elevated throughout most of the show. I have to say that he is a pretty good man to go through all of that for me to watch another man perform, but I'm glad he did. This was my favorite show and my most memorable experience. The atmosphere was really nice and it was smaller and more personal as compared to previous shows that I attended. He also, in my opinion, looked better than he had ever looked on that night. He was dressed in a long, red velvet jacket through most of the show which eventually changed to black.

As I was mesmerized by each performance, something happened that I will never forget. There was a set of stairs on the side of the stage that we were sitting on. About half way through the show, during his performance of "What Are You Doing New Years Eve," down he came. He began to dance with a fan that I thought handled herself really well. She stayed very calm. He began to work his way down the side of the theater. He started to sing to a teenage girl and kissed her hand. She, too, kept it together. He proceeded to sing to an elderly woman about four rows in front of me. He also kissed her hand.

I remember Bryce looking at me over and over to see my expression as he came closer and closer to us. I know he was wondering what I would do or how I would react if he made it up that far. This is something that I will never know because he left through a side door to the right of us.

A few feet away is probably the closest I will ever get to my idol. Every time I hear him sing that song when I am listening to that CD in my car around the holidays, I always remember that moment. Until this day, I wish it was me he was dancing with or my hand he was kissing, but I also think that everything happens for a reason. Again, you never know how you are going to react if you are put in that type of a situation. For all I know, I may have thrown up on him.

"Winners never quit and quitters
never win."
~ Vince Lombardi

"When you feel like giving up,
remember why you held on for so
long in the first place."
~ Unknown

"The creative habit is like a drug.
The particular obsession changes,
but the excitement, the thrill of your
creation lasts."
~ Henry Moore

Chapter 7
My Second Letter

After the excitement, I was also looking forward to the holidays. For Christmas, I had received a book that was just released by my idol. I had asked for it and I was really excited to get it. It was not that the book did not interest me, but I did not read it immediately. This is because at the time, life for me just seemed so busy.

I am not much of a reader unless it is required or something that interests me. I actually went to college to become an English major because I wanted to become a writer. I quickly changed my tune when I realized how much I disliked reading. I then changed my major to psychology which I thought was much more interesting. I guess the main reason why I did not open my new book was that I was trying to put some time and space between myself and my fantasy. My obsession with my idol really had started to bother me. It made me crazy and sometimes I wondered if I was crazy. Therefore, I felt that as long as he was out of sight, he was out of mind. Opening that book was like Pandora opening the box. Nothing good could come out of it without there being negative consequences of some kind.

It was a long winter and my son, Ethan, and I spent a lot of time indoors trying to stay warm and busy. I became a huge fan of the *Ellen DeGeneres Show*. Ethan and I often watched it together and sometimes he would look at me with concern when I would laugh hysterically during most of her show.

I remember there was this one week where Ellen had her fans write letters about how she could make their dreams come true. One woman wanted to meet Brody Hutzler, who played Patrick Lockhart on the soap opera, *Days of Our Lives*, and to be an extra on the show. Ellen had the woman on the show and Brody surprised her. He brought her roses. She then got to spend the whole day with him and got a chance to be an extra on the show.

I thought about how amazing it would be to be able to meet my idol and spend the day with him. As I began to contemplate actually writing a letter to Ellen, I gave myself a reality slap. After doing some soul searching, I had decided that I never wanted to meet my idol. I think at this point in my life, looking back on my obsession and how out of control I felt at times, I had decided there had to be an ending and that meant concerts, too. Even though fantasizing about my idol and going to shows had brought excitement to my life, it also seemed to be bringing on depression that I could not explain and at times I started to question my own happiness. When I separated myself from the craziness and came back to reality, I always seemed really happy.

I would joke about the depression to Maria. We started to refer to the depression as the idol withdrawals. I felt as if my idol was a really good drug that gave me a really good high and when it wore off and I felt I needed more, I couldn't always get it. Sometimes it was a terrible feeling and I did not want to feel that way anymore.

It is ironic that I would use that analogy considering I am one of the most straight laced people you will ever meet. Yes, it is true, I have never tried drugs. I have to say that I am proud of that though because there are few people out there today who can say that truthfully.

When I say that I am straight laced, in no means do I mean that I am an uptight person or even conservative. I just like to think that more times than not, I have a good head on my shoulders. I do not like to fill my body with substances that mess with my brain or my ability to have good judgment and think clearly. Don't get me wrong, I am human. Sometimes I do make mistakes, only under the influence of my own stupidity. I do realize that nobody is perfect and I do accept others for who they are and for the decisions that they make because it's their own life to live.

I also don't smoke or drink, although my dad would argue that I should have a glass of wine a day. If I drank a glass of wine right now, I would be plastered.

Taking care of my body and keeping in shape has always been important to me. I have been involved in the martial arts for about seven years with some time off in between pregnancies. I am close to going into training for my black belt.

I love getting on the elliptical and listening to my iPod. It is also a great excuse to indulge in my love for music and I am desperately trying to shed my last ten pounds of baby weight. I love Play Station Dance Revolution, but it still comes second to my Play Station Karaoke Revolution.

Although I'm a rational thinker, I can't help to be somewhat of a free spirit. I love to do things that are different or out of the ordinary. I remember when I got my belly button pierced in college, I was so afraid to let my dad know about it. He has a very old school, traditional way of thinking stemming from his pure Italian heritage as his parents were born and raised in Italy. I told him that I got a tattoo because I figured he would get really angry so the piercing would not seem like a big deal. When he found out, he told me he would have preferred that I got the tattoo. I will never forget his words, "You know who does things like that? Assholes do things like that." Bryce and I always joke about his reaction and laugh.

When it came time for the tattoo, a butterfly on the small of my back, I kept my mouth shut. Everyone knew about it but my dad. I remember going out to breakfast one Sunday morning in a small diner with David, Bryce and my dad. As the waitress was wearing a short waisted shirt, she was exposing about half of the huge tattoo that traveled across her back. My dad looked at me and said, "You'd better never do that. That looks like shit."

As David and Bryce quickly buried their heads in their breakfast dishes to hide their laughter, they may as well have thrown me under the bus. My dad caught on right away and yelled, "Jesus Christ!" Nice job, Dad, using the Lord's name in vain on a Sunday morning in the middle of a diner, where some were fresh out of church.

I had many other things in my life that were exciting, a wonderful husband, a beautiful son, a great family, a nice house and a wonderful career that I knew would be waiting for me when my kids were ready to go to school. I started to think about how sucked in I got by this reality show and how crazy it made me. Of course I would always be a huge fan but felt more of a need to stay grounded.

I had met Bryce in college. What is weird is that he was the first person I met. I introduced myself to him my first day of school as a freshman in my very first class, Spanish I. We were really good friends all four years and never dated until the April before we graduated. I actually had a really serious relationship with our friend Jude through most of college and surprisingly, we are all still good friends. I always pictured myself marrying Jude, but in the end it all worked out for the best. He married Sierra, the sister of another mutual college friend. Sierra ended up being a much better match for him than me. I must say it is a small world but I'm glad things worked out the way they did.

I know that I am lucky because there are so many people out there that are looking for the very things that I have already found. I could not ask for more but my obsessions at times made me want to be in a different place, which for me was not realistic, making me lose sight of all that was important.

I then found myself admitting to myself that as much as I would love to meet my idol, that maybe I was afraid to meet him. Sometimes you can build somebody up so much in your mind and put them on a pedestal. Then when you meet the real thing, you find out that you are disappointed. Sometimes they turn out to be not what you thought they were. Maybe it was more important to keep the dream alive.

It was like being a teenager with a really bad crush. This took me back to those not so good days in high school where you really liked someone but the feelings were not mutual. So you needed to either deal with the rejection or just face the fact that in their eyes you were just "Invisible."

Months went by before I found out that my idol was coming to the Bank of America Pavilion. I was not sure what to do. Being the weak individual that I am, I decided to feed the addiction and I bought two tickets. As if that was not bad enough, I came across two tickets to Mohegan Sun in Connecticut and did not think twice about claiming them without realizing it was the same show.

Come June, one month before the first of the two shows, I had some time on my hands and figured what better time than to break out the book that I waited six months to read. I finished the book in four nights. I guess when it rains, it pours.

The book sucked me in when I could not be any weaker, and I began contemplating another letter. I felt like I needed to express myself after reading the book. I thought that maybe it would be possible for me to deliver it to him at the show and then I could be sure that he would really get it this time. I began to handwrite the letter because I thought it may be more personal. The letter rambled on for four pages.

Dear Idol,

I just finished reading your book. Although most people would give anything to be in your shoes, living the dream, are you really living your dream? I am not concerned about you in a granny way. I am actually only four years older than you.

When I was reading your book and came to the part where you were talking about your old and new friendships, I felt really sad for you. When you explained how the people you grew up with who you thought would always be your friends and part of your life are not anymore and how the people you are friends with now are only there when you have a job for them to do, I almost wanted to come travel with you . That way when you got bored or lonely you would have someone to hang out with who actually just wanted to spend time with you. In today's world, good friends are hard to come by and you are lucky to have just one.

I know that your real passion and dream is to be in the classroom. Just knowing that your heart is in the right place is an inspiration alone to all of your fans. Although I would be sad if I could only listen to one CD, I think it is important for you to be happy.

My one question is, can you ever really go back? I have this vision of you waking up in the morning to get ready for work, driving to the school that you will work at with hundreds of screaming fans chasing you into the building.

I worked with special education students while I was working to get my certification and Master's degree in guidance counseling. I agree that this profession is rewarding. I formed many close bonds with those kids, many of which I still have today.

I know you think that God put you where you are for a reason and in your given circumstance, I think your idea about raising money to help YMCA's around the world to develop programs to help special needs kids is a great idea. I drive by our YMCA every day on the way to work and I often think of you. I decided to pick up a brochure for you with some contact information. They already have a program for special education students but I am not sure to what extent.

I am embarrassed to say that this is not my first letter to you. I wrote you a letter in 2003 and tried to be slick by sending it to an address that I thought was your mother's. I'm not sure you ever received it.

I am here tonight to enjoy your show and will also be at your August 28th show in Boston. I have enclosed two poems that I like to read whenever I have a bad day. I thought they would be helpful to you when you are having one of those days where you just want to give up.

Although there are times when I am sure you just want to get away from it for a while, there must be some good perks to your new life. If leaving it all behind is what you really want then I will say prayers that it will happen for you. No matter what you decide, your true fans should only want for your happiness.

For Today

For today, I will embrace life.
For today, I will make the best of my circumstances.
For today, I will celebrate the joy of simple things.
For today, I will learn something new.
For today, I will be a better person.

For today, I will reach out to someone in need.

For today, I will be thankful.

For today, I will dream with my eyes open.

For today, I will laugh.

For today, I will encourage a friend.

For today, I will use my imagination.

For today, I will relax.

For today, I will listen.

For today, I will take time...

To Achieve Your Dreams Remember Your ABC's

Avoid negative sources, people, places, things and habits.

Believe in yourself.

Consider things from every angle.

Don't give up and don't give in.

Enjoy life today, yesterday is gone, tomorrow may never come.

Family and friends are living treasures, seek them and enjoy their riches.

Give more than you planned to.

Hang on to your dreams.

Ignore those who try to discourage you.

Just do it.

Keep trying no matter how hard it seems, it will get easier.

Love yourself first and most.

Make it happen.

Never lie, cheat or steal, always strike a fair deal.

Open your eyes and see things as they really are.

Practice makes perfect.

Quitters never win and winners never quit.

Read, study and learn about everything important in your life.

Stop procrastinating.

Take control of your own destiny.

Understand yourself in order to better understand others.

Visualize it.

Want it more than anything.

Xcellerate your efforts.

You are unique of all Gods creations, nothing can replace YOU.

Zero in on your target and go for it.

By Wanda Carter Hope

I sealed the letter in an envelope and paper-clipped it to the inside of a purple YMCA brochure that provided some information to help with his plan for YMCAs around the world to give children with disabilities the same opportunities as regular education children. How mint of me to think of that, huh?

On July 29th, four days after my thirty-first birthday, Bryce and I drove to Mohegan Sun to meet up with Aunt Carol and Uncle Tony. We met them in the parking garage and Aunt Carol giggled and said, "Look at you all dressed up for him." I wasn't dressed glamorously but

I did want to look my best that night. I wore a fitted shirt with jeans and just a little bit of make up because sometimes less is more.

Bryce and Uncle Tony planned on making a night of it in the casino while Aunt Carol and I went to the show. Beforehand, we had a nice dinner. However, the anticipation of the show made it hard for me to enjoy much of a meal. When Aunt Carol and I left Bryce and Uncle Tony behind at the restaurant as a start to guys' night out, we made our way to the arena for our girls' night out.

After passing through security, we made our way to the souvenir line which was incredibly long. Standing in line gave us the opportunity to check out other fans that were also waiting. It was hard not to notice one woman standing next to me who was old enough to be my mother. She had on these homemade earrings with my idol's face on them. She had on a t-shirt from a previous concert and a homemade bag with all kinds of pictures. After getting through the crowd, I bought a bucket hat, a license plate and a program.

We then made our way to our seats. I was looking everywhere for the bodyguard who had made himself visible at the last two shows. I was thinking that I could possibly slip him my letter. It was absolutely hopeless and the place was absolutely huge, bigger than I had pictured. I was ready to pocket the letter and call it quits. Then, Aunt Carol asked one of the ushers if it would be possible to get a letter to my idol, something that I never would have done on my own. Thank you, Aunt Carol. He was very anxious to bring us back to security.

A young girl took the brochure from me and took the letter and felt it. She looked at me and said, "No anthrax, right?" I was shocked and told her no. I guess they can never be too careful, though. She said that my letter would definitely get to him. I was still doubtful but I figured it was either that or bring the letter home with me, after I spent so much time and effort writing.

As we walked to our seats, I got really excited because we were really close. Behind us, there were two more women about my mother's age, with the homemade bags. Another woman sat behind us with her husband, who slept through the entire show.

The show was again, excellent, but there was one drawback. Wouldn't it figure that the largest woman sat right in front of me? Every time my idol made it over to our side of the stage, she would jump up screaming and waving while I, five foot nothing, could see not a thing. Lucky for me, she and her friend left after intermission.

When the show came to an end and we were leaving the arena, Aunt Carol had commented jokingly to the woman behind us about her husband sleeping through the whole show. I guess she had dragged him there as I had dragged Bryce so many times. She was just happy that he took her.

Although the show was fantastic, this was the show that left me the most depressed. Not only did I realize that I forgot to enclose a check in my letter as a contribution to his new foundation, which was part of my slick plan, but I was really counting on a response this time. At the time, I believed that my letter was not the usual fan letter and I thought he may think it was special. I guess every fan wants to think that his or her letter is more special than all the rest. Again, how totally awesome of me for being a complete jackass?

I began to feel very angry, for absolutely no reason, but I could not help the way that I was feeling. Then the questions in my head started. Did he get it? Was it just another fan letter to him? Did he appreciate it? Is he just too busy to respond to fan letters? Am I an idiot?

Again, I vented to both Elizabeth and Maria about the situation and they told me not to take it personally. I was so sad and I was not even sure that I wanted to attend the next show in Boston. I did not know if I should just leave it alone. Or, if I did attend the show in Boston, should I try again?

Elizabeth reassured me that he did receive it and appreciated it, but no matter how he felt when he read it, he probably would not respond because he receives hundreds of letters and has no clue who I am. I knew deep down that was all true. I did not want to hear this because I had never wanted to be realistic about it. I just wanted this dream I had to come true even if I knew it was impossible. I felt that if I hoped enough that my fantasy would become a reality. Who is to say that it could never happen?

I decided to go to the next show, enjoy it and stop thinking so irrationally. I think I had started to actually irritate myself with my unrealistic expectations and stupidity.

"To succeed in life, you need three things:
a wishbone, a backbone and a funnybone."
~ Reba McEntire

"The greatest pleasure in life is doing what people
say you cannot do."
~ Walter Bagehot

"There is no telling how many miles you will have
to run while chasing a dream."
~ Unknown

Chapter 8
A Third Attempt

In getting ready to attend what I decided would be my last show for a while, I wondered if I should leave well enough alone. Or, should I make one more attempt to connect with my idol. If nothing else, at least I could forward my contribution.

Giving a donation was something that I definitely planned to do. Frankly, I knew if the check cleared, then I finally could no longer make excuses for my idol not responding because he did not get the letter. At least I would know that he was not responding because either he would not or could not for the most obvious of reasons.

On Sunday morning, August 28th, Bryce drove me to Maria's house in Abington. She would be attending the concert with me. After Bryce dropped me off, we hung out for a while before we went to the show. I remember it being very uncomfortable because she was having some marital problems and her husband for some reason blamed me because he knew she talked to me about things. I never quite understood that. Maria did talk to me about quite a bit and I knew that she was not happy. As I always listened and was always there for her, I never gave her a lot of advice because truthfully, she never took it. She always did what she wanted, which I respect. The only advice I remember giving her that she ever took was to try to talk about things and to try counseling because they had two children together. Unfortunately, it did not work.

We got ready to go and left early because with Boston's Big Dig, there was no telling how long it would take us to get there. We had no problems and ended up getting there two hours before the doors even opened.

We walked to a small restaurant and we were seated on the back deck overlooking the Boston Harbor. As it should have been very relaxing, I was experiencing a lot of pre-show jitters and anxiety. You would think that I was the one who was performing. We finally decided to make our way down to the Pavilion.

Once again, I found myself looking at the hundreds of fans that were waiting outside, hoping it would not rain. We walked by one girl who was around the age of sixteen. She was holding several signs. As she noticed us trying to read what her signs said, she yelled at us, "I have no shame!" I thought to myself, oh my. We were absolutely speechless. We looked at each other and started to laugh. We were not judging her but just trying to read what her signs said and she totally freaked out. Love and luck to the *Obsessive Irrational Fan*. It is when I experience this type of fan that I do not feel so bad about my own craziness. Later, we saw her down by the front row. Now, why am I not surprised?

Before leaving for the show, I had foolishly decided to make a third attempt. I had purchased a small gift for my idol, a miniature book with words of inspiration from famous people and an astrology kit tied together with a yellow ribbon. Inside the small book was my check with the following note:

Dear Idol,

Thank you for all of the great music in the last two years. You have brought excitement to my life as I'm sure your fans bring excitement into yours.

I left you a letter inside a purple YMCA brochure on July 29th when you performed at Mohegan Sun and realized that I forgot to enclose my contribution to your foundation. Enclosed is my donation.

Here are some things to keep you busy for the rest of your tour. I know that it is impossible for you to respond to your fans but I hope you get this and I hope that you got my letter.

Good luck on the rest of your tour. I am looking forward to your upcoming CD and Christmas tour.

We approached a girl wearing a blue Bank of America Pavilion shirt sitting in a circular booth. She looked really nice and I was looking for someone who seemed approachable. I asked her who I could give my gift to so that I could get it to my idol. I knew it was possible because of my last experience at Mohegan Sun with Aunt Carol. The girl told me to come around to the door where there was another lady who did not look so friendly. She said in a very panicky tone, "Please do not enter the booth," and was all freaked out, you know, because I am so scary. Anyway, she started yelling at me and telling me that there was no way to get anything to him and told me to go away. I did not know if I was going to cry or punch her, but with my excellent ability to control my explosiveness, I remained calm, and was determined to find someone else to help me.

In a large way, I was a little hesitant to approach anyone with the way I was just treated by the scary monster lady. Then, a nice gentleman with a maroon shirt labeled STAFF pointed me in the right direction.

I handed my gift to a young girl with blonde hair sitting at the entrance of the gate for all those lucky fans that actually had backstage passes. She was very nice and handed it off to a guy wearing a Boston Red Sox shirt who brought it backstage. After seeing the Sox shirt, being the big Sox fans that Bryce and I are, in a weird way, I had a sense that I could trust him. I was very happy and then I started thinking back on what had happened to me a few moments earlier at the circular booth with the witch lady and thought to myself, what a huge bitch. There was a big piece of me that wanted to go back there just to let her know that I got my gift to him, to slap a big L on her forehead and say how do you like those apples!

The show was as enjoyable as it could be since I already saw the show once before. As I am always up for a show with my idol, just to know that I am in the same vicinity as him, I do not really know how groupies can go from show to show to watch the same performance over and over.

Well, this was it for me. I knew that I needed to come to grips with the fact that there would really never be any contact between myself and my idol. At least I knew that if the check cleared that the book had been opened and it got to the right place. To me, it would be at least some sort of closure which would be the beginning to an end.

On September 13th, twelve days after the tour ended, the check did clear. I, of course, have not gotten a response and still remain with many unanswered questions that frequently enter my mind. I guess in playing the role of the fan, I will never really know the truths I am looking for regarding stardom and as far as expectations, what is unreasonable. I knew that someday, I would be able to make peace with my situation and I would better accept that my wish upon this star would never be granted.

"Learn from yesterday, live for today, hope for tomorrow."
~ Unknown

"Every new beginning comes from some other beginning's end."
~ Seneca

Chapter 9

Three Years Later:
Out with the Old & In with the New

It's been three years since my last attempt to somehow connect with my idol and since then a lot has happened in my life. In 2006, I gave birth to a beautiful baby girl who we named Faith Leahnetta. Leahnetta was my grandmother's name. Now with two little ones, there need not be any wondering about how busy life has been.

I had attended a Christmas show in 2005 at the Orpheum Theater in Boston which I almost missed due to another difficult pregnancy. As I looked forward to my up close and personal performances by my still famed favorite, I struggled to get there. I choked down a soft pretzel to stop the nausea as I waited in line for my Collectible Christmas ornament and my program.

The show was very different from the last Christmas show that we attended. It was more like a play that was supposedly scripted with the help of my idol. It started off with a grumpy old lady who had lost the Christmas spirit and it was a little boy who was her neighbor who ended up bringing the joy back into her life. All the songs revolved around the plot. It was really cute but I still preferred the last year's show over this one. My idol seemed more of a part of a cast and even though I did get to look at him and hear his unbelievable voice, he did not interact at all with the audience until the end of the show. I felt like it was not as personal as his other shows. The show also started an hour late due to technical difficulties but I made it through and still enjoyed every minute of it.

It seemed as if it took a long time for the release of his new CD. I had read something about him not being happy with it and then removing songs from it, leaving four originals and the rest being covers. At this time, my idol was the victim of some controversy that had taken place on *Live with Regis and Kelly* and rumors were flying around that he was gay. There was no tour that year and it seemed as if he was fading for a while. As he finally released his CD in fall of 2006, in order to promote his CD, he started to make himself a little more public again. I was disappointed that there was no tour and no actual Christmas tour but Bryce and I were able to catch a Christmas show in Hartford, one of the few selected cities that he would be performing in that year.

I enjoyed the show as the atmosphere was great and there was a lot of humor in the show. My idol openly joked about the media previous to the show and it was quite funny. Shame on you, Kelly Ripa.

In 2007, I attended another Christmas concert at Mohegan Sun. Bryce and I took the trip with my mom and dad. Bryce and my dad enjoyed the casino and my mom and I went to the show. Although the performance was good, he seemed to be somewhat out of steam. He did not interact much with his fans but most of the hour and a half stood in one spot behind the microphone and just sang. This seemed very out of character for him considering I had seen him several times before. This was a quite different experience. After the show, I had heard that he was somewhat under the weather. It probably took everything out of him just to go out there under the lights and put his full effort into the singing part, which is never a disappointment. His encore was unbelievable. I remember getting goose bumps from the power in his voice as he sang the song "All Is Well."

This was the last show I had attended before my idol surrendered to Broadway. As I would have loved to see him on Broadway, New York City was not in the playing cards for a mother of two.

In 2008, I was excited to find out during a new season of *American Idol* that he was releasing a new CD. This was surprising because there had been no mention of it and I would never have expected him to be working on a new CD while he was on Broadway. Naturally, I bought it the day it was released but I was beginning to feel that the excitement was not there like it used to be. It was like when you are in a new relationship and everything seems so exciting and new, but then as you get used to each other the excitement wears off a little. At first I thought it was because I was just tired physically from raising two children, but then started to realize that for a while now, what once seemed to be a crazy obsession was becoming more of a distant thing of the past.

I remember going for a drive in the car with Bryce, Ethan and Faith, just for a ride to nowhere, something that we do frequently. As my kids thoroughly enjoy music and are used to listening to what I listen to in the car day after day, Ethan always requests to hear

"Falling," which is undoubtedly his favorite. Lately, it always requires me to take out the CD that I am currently enjoying.

As the four of us were driving, he proceeded to ask for the same song per usual. As I took out the CD I looked at Bryce and said, "I think I'm all Clayed out." There are no words to describe the look on Bryce's face when those words came from my mouth but he did say that he thought that, "Jesus was going to fall out of the sky." The truth is I think J.C. did fall from the sky, but not that one.

I always tuned into *American Idol* since season two. Season four won me as a true fan to a new born country star, Carrie Underwood, who I saw at Foxwoods in August 2008. I am always excited to go to a concert, as long as I am a fan of the music. I love everything from the hype to the atmosphere to the actual performance. Carrie was blessed with an unbelievable voice and I am envious of her. She is also, without a doubt, one of the most beautiful women in country music.

Seasons three and six left me somewhat disappointed although I still had some favorites from season five such as Chris Daughtry and Kellie Pickler.

Although I would always continue to be a true fan of Clay Aiken, my most admired idol, I began to accept that the excitement and enthusiasm of my fandom, once strongly possessed and sought after for the last five years, had finally been grounded….and then something happened.

2004
Clay Aiken Measure of a Man Tour
Ryan Center, URI

"Life is not measured by the number
of breaths we take, but by the moments
that take our breath away."
~ Unknown

"All I know is that you love me...
in my dreams."
~ Unknown

PASSION

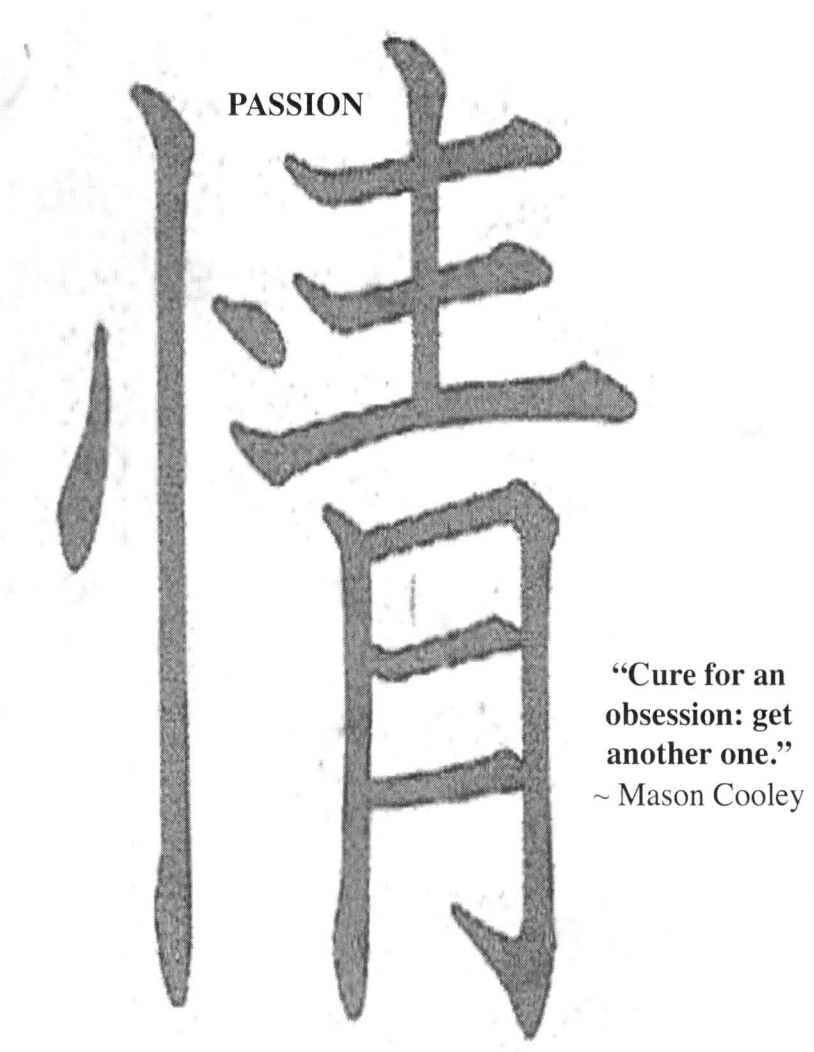

"Cure for an
obsession: get
another one."
~ Mason Cooley

Chapter 10
American Idol *(Season 7)*

As a new year surfaced, so did a new season of *American Idol*. I found myself watching week after week, looking forward to every Tuesday and Wednesday, carefully planning my schedule around shows because it would be a tragedy if I missed it. This season held the most talent that I had ever seen. I watched quietly, trying to hide my newest secret. Without words and large efforts to cover any expressions, I tried to stay subtle.

Some of my thoughts and feelings were both very similar but also very different from my past infatuation with season two runner up, Clay Aiken.

One of the major differences was that I was actually more embarrassed because three months into the show, I realized that my most recent crush was for a twenty-one year old and wondered if that was wrong, being thirteen years older. Being a thirty-four year old mother of two and having no more than an innocent crush on someone I knew I would never even come close to meeting, I was still feeling this weird guilt.

I started to think back on the high school student who had the crush on me that I said seemed icky. As I realized that there was an eleven year difference between this student and me, I found myself thinking in a whole different light. I then started to feel extremely guilty. I did think there was a big difference between a seventeen year old and a twenty-one year old but I felt the need to get things off my chest. I needed to hear from someone else that I wasn't some weirdo. I picked up the phone and called Maria.

As I began to try to bring up the subject, I almost automatically felt uneasy about talking with her and confiding in her. We had drifted a little since her divorce. She had a new love interest, whom she had been dating for two years, and I still had not met him. I feared that our friendship had started to go in two different directions. I was desperately looking for someone to make me feel better about what was going on in my head. As she was going through a different time in her life, I felt that we were in different places and that we no longer had the same things in common. Her tone made me feel like she did not really want to be bothered talking about something so beneath her.

When I started to talk about the new season of *American Idol*, a show which she initially got me interested and involved in, she immediately turned the conversation in a different direction with her quick response of, "I don't really watch that any more because Brad doesn't watch it." I truly believe that she boycotted the show midway through season four when the love of her life, Constantine Maroulis, was voted off prematurely. Now that I think about it, I remember how steaming mad she was. She did say she was never watching the show again.

As I knew I was on my own with this one, I then started to try to justify things myself and came up with ten reasons why what was going on in my head was okay:

1. Billy John & Katie Lee – 32 year age difference
2. Catherine Zeta Jones & Michael Douglas – 25 year age difference
3. Donald Trump & Melania Knauss – 24 year age difference
4. Harrison Ford & Calista Flockhart – 22 year age difference
5. Tom Cruise & Katie Holmes – 16 year age difference
6. Demi Moore & Ashton Kutcher – 15 year age difference
7. Seal & Heidi Klum – 11 year age difference
8. Brad Pitt & Angelina Jolie – 11 year age difference
9. Mariah Carey & Nick Cannon – 10 year age difference
10. Jim Carrey & Jenny McCarthy – 10 year age difference

Need I say more? After all, age is just a number.

Where normal everyday people would get looked at with disapproval for this, celebrities easily get away with dating outside of their generation with no questions asked.

As each week passed, I began downloading the newest song to a CD. I figured that if he did not get a recording contract that I would at least be able to have a CD with as many songs as I could get until he got voted off the show. I must have trashed at least six CDs by the end of it all. I guess that I could have just waited until it was the end for him and downloaded them all together, but that was not even an option because

I looked forward to having that new song to add to the group to listen to in the car that following week. My new idol made it to the number four spot, allowing my final CD to contain twelve songs, twelve bucks well spent on iTunes.

I also went onto the *American Idol* website and downloaded some pictures so that I could make my own personal CD cover and label. I put a picture of my new favorite on my cell phone as a screen saver. I tried to get Bryce to download one of his songs from the show as a ring tone but none of them were available. At the end of it all, I somehow ended up being a member of laughaholics, some funnies that somehow get texted to my phone everyday. I cannot seem to get rid of it.

It had been five years since I had attended an *American Idol* concert. Although I had been tuning in every year, as I said, I was never really interested enough to actually get myself to buy tickets for a show. Then, *American Idols Live* was to be held at The DCU Center.

When it came the morning for tickets to go on sale, I had been away from the computer and realized the night after, oh shit… the tickets. I ran downstairs hoping that I could still get good seats, which was a very unrealistic thought. There were only crappy seats left and I was determined to get the best seats I possibly could without spending a crazy amount of money. I went to some ticket broker sites online. To get decent seats, it was one hundred forty five dollars a ticket, more than twice the original face value. I felt that if I was going to spend sixty eight dollars for crappy seats, I didn't mind spending one hundred and forty five for decent ones. In the end, it cost close to four hundred dollars after shipping and convenience fees. So yes, I did spend a crazy amount of money, and yes, this is absolutely ridiculous, but oh, so worth it in the end.

The night before the show, I found out that one of our best friend's parents, Marilyn and Gerome, had VIP seats and backstage passes because they were acquainted with one of the idol favorites, Michael Johns. I knew that I had no chance of meeting my idol because you can't transfer passes, but I was hopeful for an autograph.

We arrived at the show early, at about six o'clock, to get my program and my eight by ten photo. I had a lot of anxiety because I did not know where Marilyn and Gerome's seats were located. I wanted to be able to find them so that I could pass off my program and eight by ten photo to them for a possible autograph. I did not know if they would be meeting the idols before or after the show and I knew that if I did not find them that my chances of getting even an autograph would be as good as gone. Getting the autograph meant so much to me because I knew that realistically it would probably be the closest thing I would ever get to meeting him.

As we found our seats, we ran into our friends Jude and Sierra. It was so funny because five years ago the four of us met at the same place for *American Idols Live, Season Two*. That's right, that was the year I foolishly thought that on my birthday I would meet Clay Aiken. Insert laughter here!

As we were all having a conversation, I kept looking around for Marilyn and Gerome and now that I am thinking about it, they probably thought I was acting weird or even maybe a bit rude. I was in luck because I finally caught sight of Marilyn and Gerome and I took off like a bullet, again rude. They were actually seated in the same section as us, which by the way were pretty good seats. I remember Bryce saying,

"These are the best seats I have ever had at a show."

I said in response, "They should be for what I paid for them."

Then he asked, "What? How much did you pay for them?"

My response was, "Never mind." I was now going to have to prepare myself for the ass ripping I was going to get for the crazy amount of money I spent on the tickets. Gladly, nothing was ever said.

Anyway, I was able to pass off my program and my picture to Marilyn and Gerome, as they were meeting with all of the idols after the show, the luckiest people ever.

As the show began, I was so excited. They started with the number ten contestant and worked their way down, each contestant singing three songs. I thoroughly enjoyed all of them and of course they decided to have an intermission right before my favorite hit the stage. It was alright because I was starving and it gave me a chance to get some food since I skipped dinner to get to the show early. I had so much anxiety waiting in the snack line. It seemed to take forever and if I did not make it back to my seat when the show started back up again, nobody was going to want to be in my way.

I also felt like the break was good because, as it never fails, we had the biggest group of tools sitting in front of us. Through the entire show, they kept getting up for beers and would come back double fisted. They were so loaded and obnoxious and I was getting really irritated. Who the hell gets trashed at an *American Idol* concert? It's a family show for cryin' out loud!

As I did make it back in plenty of time, unfortunately, so did the ensemble in front of us who continued to get up and come back several times for their frequent bathroom breaks after drinking two beers every ten minutes.

I was excited to watch my idol perform but he was a little off that night. I wondered if he was sick or even losing his voice a bit. I felt that although he only performed three songs, it seemed to go by so fast. I regretted not bringing my camera. As in most shows, I could always remember the performances so clearly and could always remember what they were wearing but for some reason it was like a complete blur to me. I think what happened was that I was so focused on his face and so taken by the sound of his voice that I didn't remember a freakin' thing.

As runner up, David Archuletta rose up through the stage playing piano and singing John Lennon's "Imagine." The crowd erupted. There were tons of Archuletta fans. Bryce and I were laughing because there was a woman who was going absolutely nuts about four rows down from us who was easily in her forties. I thought she was going to come out of her skin. What was even funnier was the

107

forty something year old gentleman who then walked up our aisle with a homemade David Archuletta t-shirt.

The one thing I will never forget was the outstanding performance by David Cook. He was definitely one of the most genuine *American Idol* winners. I remember watching the show week after week and Simon calling him arrogant. What really bothers me about this is that the judges tell the performers they need to have confidence and then when they have it, all of a sudden they are deemed arrogant. As I mostly agree with Simon's opinions when it comes to singing, I totally disagreed with this comment.

I also disagreed with his comment about Carly Smithson not dressing well. She was another one of my season seven favorites. Mr. Man Boobs himself, with the black t-shirt he wears on every show, as he should appear in a daily animated cartoon, should not be giving fashion advice to anyone. If I remember correctly, it was him five years ago who said with his English accent, "This is a singing competition!"

As I watched David Cook perform that night, it was obvious that he is just a natural performer. At one point during his performance, he came to the side of the stage that we were sitting on and there were a couple of teenage girls trying to take his picture. When he completely acknowledged them by pointing and smiling at them, they looked at each other, mouths wide open screaming.

It was such a great example of what kind of an overwhelming feeling a fan gets when they are actually acknowledged, individually picked out in the crowd. Although he didn't know them, he probably made there night more special than he could ever imagine. I will most definitely be purchasing the new David Cook CD when it is released.

When I went home that night, I was so excited. I was anxiously awaiting a phone call in the morning from Marilyn, but at the same time I didn't want to get my hopes up.

I usually do not have that kind of luck, in a way, I guess I kind of did that night. When Marilyn called, she told me she got me the top five contestants' autographs along with Michael Johns, who finished eighth in the competition. She also got my eight by ten signed. I was so excited because I did not expect all of those autographs. I was just hoping for the one, hoping that she could get close enough to just get the one.

She also got personal pictures with most of them and she had them made for me. After looking at the pictures, I noticed that my idol was wearing a white denim jacket and jeans. It still did not ring any bells to me other than the hair being tied half back. The truth is that I was so enthralled with just being in the same room with him that night that I don't think I would have noticed if he was not wearing anything at all. Okay, yes I would!

In truth, I have never been attracted to any man for his body. It is actually always the last thing that I notice. I have always seemed to be attracted to taller thinner men. I always notice a face first. Smile and teeth are always important followed by eyes and hair. To me, there is nothing sexier than a man who can sing. Playing an instrument is another plus. The most important things, of course, are sense of humor and personality because without that, none of the other things really matter. They are irrelevant.

I once met a guy on the Spirit of Boston cruise when I was at an anniversary party for my Auntie Beverly and Uncle Rick. It was a great time. I noticed him right away because he was absolutely perfect, like a Ken doll. As we exchanged information, I found out that he went to a local college in Boston and was from Ohio. We actually got together a couple of times but the minute he opened his mouth, he was actually quite ugly. Needless to say that didn't work. It doesn't matter how beautiful you are, it's what is on the inside that counts. It's not that he was a bad guy, but we just had very different personalities, senses of humor and very different ideas about life.

Marilyn then proceeded to tell me that she actually had a lengthy conversation with my favorite idol. As I listened to her with envy, she told me that he had the most gorgeous eyes, which I knew but would have loved to experience. What a tease. I had asked her if he was sick or losing his voice and she said no, but as she approached him the first thing that he said to her was "I am so tired." She said that they were all so exhausted, mentally and physically, and that she felt bad for them. As she has three sons of her own, she gave him a hug. She said that shockingly, he actually squeezed her when he hugged her back, seeming so homesick. She said he was one of the most down to earth and nicest people that she ever met. I came very close to asking her what he smelled like but I thought that may be crossing the line.

I immediately went shopping for frames for my new pictures. I keep them on my nightstand as I frequently get the head shake or the eye roll from my husband. I often think about the fact that he actually had to touch that picture to sign it. Therefore, I don't let anyone else touch it.

I was so excited about my news and so excited to share it with someone that I again attempted to call Maria. As she answered the phone she sounded very unenthusiastic to speak with me. I guess I should have taken the hint then, but being as excited as I was, I began to tell her about the show and how Marilyn and Gerome had gotten all of the autographs for me and how exciting it was. Her response was, "Yeah, I guess it's exciting, if you're into that."

At that moment I grew sad when I realized that she had become a different kind of friend, the friend that had really become more of an acquaintance. What's a friend for if you can't talk to them about your passions and the things that you get excited about? As I am still hurt by her reaction to my news, I guess I can't expect everyone to have the same passions as I do. I do believe though that she could have been a little more enthusiastic, even if she wasn't "into it." I started to miss my old friend. Someday, I hope to have her back. One of my favorite quotes says it best: "In order to have a friend, you need to be a friend."

As the excitement started to wear off a little I was able to reflect on some of the things that Marilyn had told me about her conversation with my idol.

When the final weeks of *American Idol* neared, there were speculations about my idol actually wanting to be voted off the show. I am not sure if that was the plan or not but I definitely think that he was feeling some extreme pressure and was not comfortable with it.

Because of his laid back personality, I think he started experiencing what I have been referring to all along as the "dream" that isn't really the "dream." I'm sure a lot of this great life experience that most people will never get an opportunity to even come close to was in fact a wonderful experience. But when do you reach a point where you've "had enough?" I believe that some people are made for this type of lifestyle, and I am also pretty sure that most of us are not. The truth is, when you really love to do something that actually seems as though it is becoming more of a chore, is it really enjoyable anymore?

I sensed that my new idol was the type of person that would much prefer the behind the scenes type of fame. Although the show was a chance of a lifetime and a great experience, perhaps it was more of a sacrifice for exposure. Maybe it is possible to capture a fan base big enough for a promising future career to be able to create and perform music at a more comfortable pace. This might be more suitable for us ordinary, down to earth and sometimes even camera shy people.

I felt that if I was on the right path, I could understand his way of thinking and I started to answer some of my wonders about stardom. As a lot of my past thoughts and questions began to resurface, I remembered my mind going through the same vicious cycle as when I was so into Clay. I always had that constant urge to meet with him and pick his brain about the change from normalcy to Hollywood craziness. In my attempts for answers, I always ended up disappointed and so I had decided that I was all set with fan letters. On the other hand, I started to reconsider an idea that I had earlier.

2008
American Idols Live Tour
DCU Center   Worcester, MA

Jason Castro

Michael Johns

Carly Smithson

2008
American Idols Live Tour
DCU Center   Worcester, MA

Brooke White   Syesha Mercado

David Cook

"If it were not for hopes, the heart would break."
~ Thomas Fuller

"I don't dream at night, I dream all day; I dream for a living."
~ Steven Spielberg

"Life is what happens to you
while you are busy making
other plans."
~ John Lennon

Chapter 11
In the Hands of Ellen

I began to accept the fact that I may never get answers to my mystery questions. Then I thought, if I want answers and hope for a possible response, someone who may be able to help me, who better to ask than Ellen DeGeneres? And so, it went.

Dear Ellen,

I am writing to you to propose a great idea for your show and also in hopes of receiving an answer to a question that has been weighing on my mind for quite some time.

Living life as a celebrity, do you ever wish you could go back to being a regular person with a regular life? Is being a celebrity as glamorous as it's made out to be?

You are probably wondering why I am searching for an answer to this question. The truth is, we all grow up having this "dream" of either meeting our favorite celebrity or being one. I have always questioned if we are all setting ourselves up for disappointment and if this so called "dream" is really the type of life we want to live.

Since the fifth grade, I have always had the dream of being a recording artist. My brother played the guitar and I sang. Come high school, we let go of the dream and focused on college and a career that was more promising. I chose a future in guidance counseling hoping to make a difference in children's lives.

I began watching American Idol *at the beginning of season two. Watching the show always brought the dream back alive again. Sometimes I thought that watching the show was a safe way of living the dream through someone else living the dream that I was always afraid to follow. I found myself being a devoted fan of runner up, Clay Aiken. He inspired me to write my first fan letter ever at the age of twenty-eight, followed by two more letters. As it may sound silly, I became very discouraged when I never received a response. I guess every fan wants to believe that the right words through a letter will somehow reach the unreachable.*

In 2004, after having my first child and deciding to be a stay at home mom, I used my spare time watching your show and focusing on unanswered questions revolving around celebrities and their fans. I started putting my thoughts, feelings and questions into a book I had titled, "Reaching Out To The Stars — The Insight Of A Devoted Fan And The Search For Reason." *I wanted to express my feelings on this topic of living on the other side of the Hollywood splendor, perceptions of stardom and being a devoted fan. I ended up shelving it two years ago, unfinished.*

This past year I recorded a CD with my brother in his small condo. I like to think of it as a personal accomplishment and have comfortably reserved my dream as a much enjoyed hobby.

As I continued to tune into American Idol, *seasons three through six, I have not been enthusiastic about it until this past season, seven. Season seven left me with an overwhelming feeling of excitement*

somewhat brought on by great talents and an embarrassing crush on
Jason Castro. Because of my past experience, I decided NOT to write
him any fan letters.

I am excited to hear from you in regard to my questions and
although I have given up on the dream of being a celebrity for many
different reasons and have been discouraged of the possibility of ever
really getting to know my idol favorites, I had hope that you could bring
these dreams alive for other hopeful fans on your show. It would be
great to present true fans with the opportunity of meeting their favorite
celebrities. After all... where would celebrities be if it weren't for us fans?

I thought this may be my final attempt and my last shot at getting
my questions answered and possibly a dream or two to come true. Then
I thought, I may not ever have the life of a celebrity, I may not even
want the life of a celebrity, but it is never too late to possibly meet one.

I have always been curious and unsure about the ups and downs
of stardom and have always wondered about if I were ever offered the
chance to be there if I would take it or not. It was like I needed that one
on one chat with a star to get the answers for the closure I needed to
make sure that I had no regrets in life.

As I am almost positive that I have made all the right choices,
I will always hope and dream of meeting a celebrity, and not just any
celebrity, but one that I am a great fan of.

I then started to think about what it might be like to be on *The
Ellen DeGeneres Show*, sitting with and meeting Ellen, Clay and Jason.

There I was, sitting in the opposite chair of Ellen. I was surprised as she introduced first Clay and then Jason to the stage. I was living any fan's fantasy. This was great because I realized that any time I wanted to add a little excitement to my life, I could come and hang out with my two favorite celebs. As they talked to me, they explained that even though celebrity status was great they wished that every now and then they could take a step back and enjoy life as it used to be. I told Clay that he could come over to the house with his significant other and the kids could play together.

As for Jason, I will be taking him to the beach. This is because when he was on the show *American Idol* he said that he liked the beach and wished he could spend more time there. That is one thing that we do have in common. I also love the beach, but what happens on the beach stays on the beach. Then, I woke up.

Even though it may be, again, a far fetched idea, I started to see things a little more clearly and I realized that it really would be a dream come true. This is because I would be fulfilling something I had always wanted in my life, to keep the life that I had now but to be sitting in an atmosphere surrounded by three people who have all had a great influence on my life. Not just any three people but one who made me want to revisit a time in my life and to be something that I am not necessarily cut out for leading. Another, who made me realize that I am happy with what I have but still find time to accomplish what I dream of at my own pace along with excitement and fantasy. Lastly, one who could make all my dreams come true, who I let into my home everyday because nowadays, it is extremely necessary to have a sense of humor and be able to laugh at the simplest of things. What would life be without laughter?

Although this is another dream that will probably never come true, writing my letter to Ellen started me thinking again and inspired me to finish writing my book. Sometimes, on the way to a dream you get lost and find a better one.

"Reality is negotiable."
~ Tim Ferris

"Imagination is the one weapon in the war against reality."
~ Jane Wagner

Chapter 12
October People

As I was driving down Malden Street for a ride in the car with the kids, I decided to try to get back in touch with the roots where it all began. I miraculously ejected my Jason Castro CD and decided to listen to my Clay Aiken *Measure of a Man* CD. Listening, I began to smile as it quickly took me back in time to a place where I used to be. I knew that even though the obsession was not what it used to be, I would always have a "thing" for Clay Aiken.

As I seemed to be in a world of my own, my cell phone began to ring. It was Bryce. As we said our good mornings, he said in a sarcastic tone, "What are you listening to?"

I asked him why, at first assuming he was busting on me because I was not listening to my Jason CD, a very rare occurrence. He said, "No really, what are you listening to?"

I said, "Clay...why?"

Then he said, "Did you hear?"

I asked, "Hear what?"

He responded, "Clay came out."

I responded, "Oh, okay whatever, really funny."

I really thought that he was teasing me because this was not the first time that he joked about Clay being gay. Then he said, "No really, it's all over the radio and he is going to be on the October issue of *People* magazine. He said that he didn't want to raise his son thinking that he had to lie or hide things." He then had my attention.

As I cannot explain how I was feeling in my complete moment of silence it was as if someone had just told me that dreams and fantasies could no longer exist.

I finally said, "Are you serious?"

He was actually sincere when he said, "Yeah, Sweetie. I wanted to tell you before you heard because I knew you were going to be crushed." I then said, "No, not really. I think I'm actually fine with it because I guess I always knew that it was a possibility."

As we said our goodbyes I continued to drive with a blank stare. My eyes filled up with tears and I quickly got myself together and called my mom who is also a fan. She, too, had already heard the news.

I continued with my daily routine and made a pit stop at Dunkin Donuts for the usual medium iced coffee with cream and sugar and some munchkins for the kids. I then returned home. My mood was very somber and depressed.

A couple of hours later I called Bryce at work. As he picked up the phone, I said, "I think I'm grieving or something."

He said, "I knew you would be."

"I really did not think this would bother me but I almost cried like three times today." He began to laugh as I was laughing too, but almost crying at the same time.

As my day went on, taking care of the kids, cleaning up and waiting for Bryce to come home, it was constantly weighing on my mind.

That night as I was cleaning up the kids toys in the family room, I started to cry. As Bryce came into the room, he asked, "What's wrong?"

I replied, "Nothing."

Bryce then said, "What is it, oh no, its not...Clay?" He started laughing and left the room as I again was laughing and crying at the same time.

I think that these laughing crying combinations were a direct vent of both feeling silly and ridiculous, but also feeling like a small piece of me had died.

It did not help that as I was cleaning up, the television in the background aired shows like *Entertainment Tonight* and *Extra* which kept showing clips over and over again of people's reactions of the Clay news. I could not help but want to slap Simon Cowell's face off his measly little neck. I always felt that Simon never liked Clay. I am not quite sure why but he has always talked about him with negative connotations.

I started to rethink the whole controversy that had happened on the *Regis and Kelly Show*. When Clay put his hand over Kelly Ripa's mouth to shut her up and she said, "I don't know where that hand has been," I'm not sure it was a homophobic comment. I honestly think he embarrassed her and she wanted to embarrass him back. To me, it seemed like she was being a little overconfident and she made herself look petty by saying that. She has been known to do the same thing to Regis several times in the past and he never made a big thing of it. I think she let her ego get the best of her. It was not becoming of her and

I always liked her until she pulled that stunt and then never apologized. At least be a big enough person to admit when you're wrong and move on.

Upon further reflection, I started to think that it was a good thing that my obsession was not as passionate. Maybe my new obsession with Jason Castro had worked as a buffer to a reaction that may have been much worse.

I had called Aunt Carol to tell her the news and because I had heard that Clay was going to be on *Good Morning America* and wanted her to find out for me when the Diane Sawyer interview was going to be on. As she had not heard the news, she had asked, "Did you really think he was not gay?"

"Well, I always knew it was a possibility but it was never really confirmed."

In truth, I never really thought he was gay until I heard about the in vitro. It was kind of a sure sign but as it was still not confirmed, I never wanted to believe it until it came from the horse's mouth. Now that it had, I guess I had to deal with the feelings that came along with it, never knowing how I really would. It's hard to anticipate a reaction to something until it actually happens and you are faced with it.

When Aunt Carol called me back, she said that the first part of the Diane Sawyer interview was already online on the *Good Morning America* website and that there would be a second part the next morning. She told me that when I told her the news, all she could think about was Uncle Tony. This is because Uncle Tony always used to tease me about my obsession with Clay. He always would refer to him as Rueben.

Uncle Tony passed away almost 4 years ago after a courageous fight with cancer. It was a very sudden diagnosis that shocked us all. He went very quickly and I can't even come to grips with the fact that he has already been gone for almost 4 years.

Uncle Tony was like a second father to me. When I married Bryce, I never felt accepted. It was always very difficult for me to deal with this. Not to sound egotistical but I never had to deal with the feeling of not being liked in my adult years. Not that I can remember, anyway. I pride myself on being a nice person and going out of my way to be there and do for others. Therefore, it never made sense to me. I have been known to forgive but to never forget. I guess that means I am a big grudge holder. I feel like forgetting about the past means that you would never learn from it, never become a stronger person, which I feel I have from many negative experiences in my life. Although things happen in life that suck, I do believe that it makes you stronger.

Aunt Carol and Uncle Tony always made me feel like part of the family. Uncle Tony and I had a special bond and sometimes I felt as if only he could understand my difficulties with people to my silly obsessions such as my love for Clay Aiken. Although he always joked, he never made me feel bad about myself for my silly hang-ups which secretly were my passions. I miss him a lot and know that if he were still here, I would have received more than one phone call so he could pick on me a little, or maybe a lot.

I tuned into The Diane Sawyer interview, parts one and two. Shortly after that, my mom delivered me the October *People*. I felt bad for Clay because even though I will never know what he was going through, I do realize that coming to grips with his sexuality and then having to tell it to the rest of the world must have been difficult. Not everyone in this world is open to homosexuality and it is because they do not understand it.

Clay is right when he said that some of his fans will not be okay with it because they won't. As a true fan, I can only speak for myself. I believe that being gay is not a choice. I think that some males are born with a female psyche and some females are born with a male psyche. There is no way of controlling that.

I am not bothered by the fact that Clay is gay per the reasoning of most people. I accept him for who he is and it doesn't change the fact that he is still a great guy with an amazing talent who will probably be a great dad. Rather, my sadness stems from the fact that there are now a lot of happy gay males out there and a lot of depressed straight females, not ever having a chance to get with Clay Aiken. The depression is all about his sexuality putting an end to the fantasy.

Funny but true, I will admit the reality of Clay coming out killed the fantasy for me for a short while. On the other hand, I was able to work through it with some deep thought and self realization. I realize that I have as much of a chance of having a slumber party with Clay Aiken as I do with Jason Castro or any other celeb for who most women fantasize. It is only a fantasy, although part of that fantasy is the hope of it possibly happening. That's what keeps us dreaming. Therefore, through it all, I guess I will just have to settle for a *Will & Grace* type of relationship with my boy Clay. I just hope that Jason is straight.

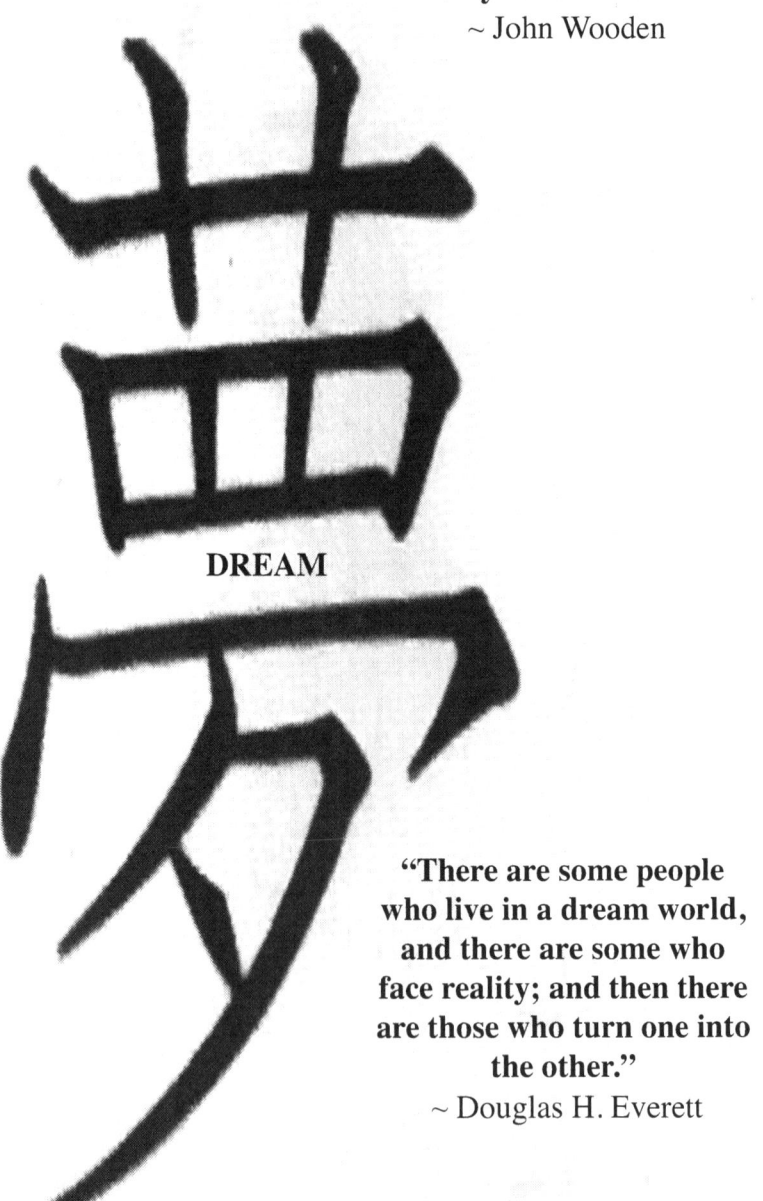

"We don't live as we wish,
but as we can."
~ Terence

"Don't let what you can't do
stop you from doing what
you can do."
~ John Wooden

DREAM

"There are some people
who live in a dream world,
and there are some who
face reality; and then there
are those who turn one into
the other."
~ Douglas H. Everett

Chapter 13
Reality and the Expectations of the Fan

For six years, I have been searching for answers to questions and feeling like the only people who could possibly give me the answers I was looking for were unreachable, untouchable…stars.

I started thinking about why we as a society get so ridiculously caught up in the celebrity scene. I wondered why it is that we get so sucked in by television shows like *American Idol*.

With my counseling background, I started to analyze some of the different possibilities of why we think the way we do based on my own personal experience, the *American Idol* experience.

I do believe that many people reach a point where they look back on their lives and wonder where they would be if they took a different path. When we admire someone excessively and refer to them as our idol or hero, is it because there is a part of us who wishes we could be where they are? Is it because deep down we once had a dream that we didn't follow through and we are envious? Three years ago, I feared that maybe I fit into this category.

When I first discovered the television show *American Idol* which started my huge obsession with Clay Aiken, it started to bring me back to a place where I once was in my life. As I revisited those times in my mind, I had some regrets about not pursuing a career as a vocalist. I suppose I never had the self esteem or the push or shove from anybody substantial in my life to follow that dream. I just thought it to be unrealistic and thought I was just young and stupid, wishing for something I felt would never happen and never really thinking I was good enough to get anywhere with it. I guess I will always wonder if I really was ever good enough. I started to feel that maybe I had missed out on something and that it was too late for me to do anything about it because I was too old and I waited too long.

As I was going through this time in my life, I decided to start singing again. I began taking some voice lessons by none other than my junior high music teacher. I thought that even though I could sing well, I didn't have an outstanding range or a lot of power. I thought that maybe there was a secret to it all that I just wasn't getting, that maybe I wasn't using my voice correctly and maybe I could learn something new and become better.

I also had my heart set on going to a recording studio and recording my own CD. I asked David if he would accompany me on acoustic guitar. David convinced me not to pay the money to go to a recording studio, that recording had been something that he had wanted to learn to do and that we could do it right in his condo. We started with the song "Underneath It All" by No Doubt, one of my favorite bands. David liked them, too.

As I was excited about my accomplishment, my brother seemed exhausted from the recording since for him it was a lot more work because he played and recorded every instrument before hand. He had said that if we did any more covers that it would have to be music we both liked because it was a lot of work and he wanted to enjoy it. Although he does like No Doubt, there were some other songs I was looking to cover that he did not like, for example, "Black Horse and the Cherry Tree" by KT Tunstall.

We had decided that our second song would be "Animal Instinct" by the Cranberries. After our third pick, Norah Jones' "Don't Know Why," he seemed to get a little more disinterested. It was like pulling teeth to get him to work a fourth which was Jewel, "You Were Meant for Me." It is my least favorite on the CD. It was right before that recording that he had told me that four songs would be it.

David had wanted to start concentrating on writing his own music and recording on his own. I was a little hurt and angry and both discouraged and sad. I was having a lot of fun and I felt as if the CD was a personal accomplishment. I did have plans to make more of it at the time. Even though I was crushed, I did understand that he had his own goals. I personally seem to think it was more important for him because he still had a chance of pursuing a career in music where in reality it was only a dream for me. He far surpassed me in musical talent and he had nothing holding him back.

I had given the CD to Bryce's cousin Laney, another who had always been supportive of me when I came into the family. She first worked at Random House and then worked her way up to a publicist in New York City. I was hoping she had some connections and could do something with it for me.

Since she liked the CD, she started telling me some of the things that I needed to do to go forward with it. It was at that moment that I realized that this was not in the cards for me. No matter how much I had dreamed of having a career in the music industry, it was just way to far from my reach, especially at this time in my life. I was married with children and not the type of person who likes change for that matter.

It took me a while to come to grips with the fact that my love for music was nothing but a most enjoyed hobby. Just as I expressed in my letter to Ellen, I finally accepted that this type of life was not for me, that I wasn't even sure if I wanted it, and it was something I needed to accept on my own. With the unanswered questions in my mind and the unanswered letters to my most admired idol from my favorite television show, I never got the closure for which I was looking.

I wondered at times if the show *American Idol* was more of an obsession than the actual crush I had on its particular artists like Clay Aiken and Jason Castro. The show itself was a means of taking a person just like me and giving them an opportunity of a lifetime, one that I never got because when I was twenty-five, the show did not exist. Then I asked myself, if it did, would I have auditioned? I don't know the answer to this question.

Between the ages of sixteen through twenty, I may have auditioned because I had more confidence, but as a twenty-one through twenty-five year old, my world was already moving in a much different direction.

I remember watching season two and the age limit being twenty-five and I was twenty-eight. I knew that auditioning was not even an option for me. Therefore, I didn't think about it much. The next year they raised the age limit to twenty-eight but I was then twenty-nine. I don't know if I looked at it as an excuse not to ever have to audition, not having the self confidence to do it anyway, or if I was irritated that I never fit into the bracket to make that decision for myself.

As a fan, always looking in from the outside and not knowing the life a celebrity actually lives from a celebrity's perspective, I will never know if this was the type of life I ever really would have wanted or if it was just the curiosity.

We, as fans, can't actually seek out a celebrity by writing to them to meet them or sit down and have a conversation with them to find out the answers to these questions. I guess I already tried that.

Then I started to realize that my experience with fandom was actually much deeper than a dream that never came true.

Does the obsession of the fan grow simply because of an emotional connection or a physical attraction to a person that we feel we know? I am sure there are some fans that definitely see the glamour rather than actually knowing or caring to know the actual person. I do believe that some of us want relationships with them because we are attracted to them physically. I think that is part of the fantasy. There is something enticing and very sexy about someone who holds a career as an actor/actress or, personally, for me, a musical artist. Would we be attracted to them if they were just an average person walking down the street in a small town? Maybe we would not. What if they were an average person who we met and got to know? Maybe we would. I am sure they want to have a relationship with someone who loves them for who they are and not just for what they can do.

This may be another reason why they steer clear of us. Do we know who they really are as a person or is it just the portrayal of an onstage artist singing to us in a dream that we wish was real. Is it the art we are in love with or the artist? Hmm, the drama of it all is intriguing.

I started to wonder if my wanting to go back to that time in my life, wanting the type of lifestyle of being a well known vocalist was an unconscious attempt to get close to these men to which I was secretly attracted. Maybe I felt I needed to have celebrity status to be friends with a star whom I thought I had a strong connection with. I started to think of my personal life as a whole.

I have had many experiences in my life where I have felt discouraged by how society works. I have experienced many negative friendships, people who only do things for others for what they can get in return, people who get more joy out of getting than giving and diminished values and morals.

What ever happened to treating people the way you want to be treated, appreciating things in life when you have to work harder for them and taking on what is referred to as responsibility?

I believe that the most important thing in life is putting others needs before your own, striving to be the best person that you can be. I truly believe that when someone dies, God will not judge them on how many Sundays they went to church but by how many things they did for others.

I started to feel that maybe I was seeking out something in my idols that I could not find within my reach. Although there are definite differences between Jason and Clay, my admiration for them is inevitable.

Clay Aiken, with his powerful voice, will give anyone listening to him goosebumps as they are sitting on the edge of their seat just waiting for him to hit the high note. When I think of the definition of an idol, I think of Clay Aiken for many reasons. Although I only know a limited version of who he may be, when I look at him I see a good person. I would be lying to say that I am not physically attracted to him and drawn to his ability as a recording artist but, more importantly, even though I only know him to an extent and that he too is not perfect, we share a lot of the same ideas and life values that I don't often see in most people. Maybe I am not as obsessed with my idol being a celebrity as I am with the excitement of the idea that there is still such a thing as good people in this world. Sometimes it bothers me that there is actually someone out there that is a lot like me and I will never get the chance to have a friendly conversation with him. To him, I am only a fan.

While reading his book, I came across a picture with a quotation that said, "My fans love to tell me funny stories. I think they see me as a friend rather than as a celebrity." I found this to be interesting because sometimes I do think of him as a friend. Unfortunately, a friendship is something that is mutual and usually goes both ways. On a more

137

positive note, I once read that "good friends are like stars…you can't always see them, but you know they are always there." Now, isn't that ironic? If I met Clay Aiken, minus celebrity status, we would probably be friends.

Jason Castro has the relaxing voice which makes you want to lay down by a fire while closing your eyes and lingering off into a "Daydream." With my latest idol crush on Jason, I felt I knew a lot less about him. He was a seventh season fourth place finisher just coming off tour with no definite promises to continue his career as a musician. I was comparing five years to one year.

Even though Jason is twenty-one years old, when I listen to his music, his soothing voice and laid back personality make me feel more relaxed about life. With his sense of humor, he makes me laugh sometimes with just an expression. He is definitely someone I feel like I could just laugh with, even if it's about nothing at all.

Some of my own questions centering on celebrity status have been answered by watching his journey through the *American Idol* dream. I also learned that I am not the only person in this world that requires more sleep than the average person.

As for the physical attraction piece, it is sometimes hard for me to talk about, never less think about. There were times when Bryce actually asked me, "If Clay Aiken knocked on your door tomorrow, would you leave me for him?" Of course, I always answered that question with a no. The part that bothered me was that I actually had to rethink that answer after I answered it. There were actual times where

I would get really moody and unbearable to be around. It was never because I didn't want to be with my husband or that I was in love with some other man, it was that I was so angry at myself for having some of the thoughts that I had been having. Being the loyal person that I have always been, never even cheating on a boyfriend, I felt an extreme amount of guilt for having had sexual thoughts and questions about whether I had truly been married to my soul mate. Of course, after a lot of thought, my answer to his question is still no.

Bryce is my best friend. After ten years of marriage it is true that a lot of the spark, passion and romance do go away. I have to believe that this is the reason that I have these fantasies. It is an innocent way of creating that excitement that isn't always there anymore. I think that this is why a lot of people cheat or get divorced. Some people feel that because that spark is gone they need to find it somewhere else. I believe that having idols and crushes on celebrities is an outlet, healthier and less dangerous than having fantasies about the guy next door. Also, after ten years of marriage, things are also changing for the better. More than the excitement of having burning passion for each other, those sparks develop into an unbelievable friendship with a person that you share the important things in life from the smiles of your children to knowing you have someone to grow old with that can overlook all of your imperfections. So then you ask yourself, which is more important? To me it is the latter. Another one of my favorite quotes says it best, "Marry someone whose soul you love, passion fades but true friendship is forever."

When I eventually came off my high with Clay Aiken and then shortly after found out he was gay, I almost felt like I was in a safe zone. Now that I knew he was gay, I felt more relieved because if my dream were to come true and I got to meet him, there would be no worries. It is never good to temp temptation.

With regard to Jason Castro, as I mentioned, I have been embarrassed about my attraction to him. This is because along with his age, his hypnotizing blue eyes and charming dreadlocks, have led me to have fantasies that I will most likely deny to most people.

When my crush started, Bryce said, in so many words, "Here we go again." I remember saying to him, "You don't have to worry because nothing could be as bad as my infatuation with Clay Aiken…and it is nowhere near that." I almost felt comfortable talking about it now knowing he was gay. The only thing that worried me was as I thought back on it, when it all started with Clay, "it was nowhere near that."

Bryce and I have often joked about the "laminated list" which is a popularized idea from the hit show *Friends* which entails a list of celebrities that a person's partner would permit them to sleep with if they were to ever meet them. Most people would not understand this unless they were familiar with *Friends*, season three episode, "The One with Frank Jr."

There was a time that Clay Aiken would have been number one on my list but would probably now be bumped to my number two by Jason Castro, followed by Tom Welling, Justin Hartley and a toss up between Robert Downey Jr. and Johnny Depp. I guess it is inevitable that I am charmed by musicians, superheroes and even pirates. Although I had thoughts about removing Clay from my list, my final decision was that he would stay.

Could being a fan be an unconscious act of persistence in defense of what feels like a rejection or a feeling of being unworthy? Three unanswered fan letters were my inspiration for writing this book. I am a rational person and realize that we cannot expect celebrities to write or email a response to every one of the hundreds of letters that they get everyday, but what can we expect? Sometimes no response at all feels like an act of ignorance even though that is not how it's supposed to come across.

Writing a letter is a personal act of reaching out to someone. Not getting a response, even though it may be an irrational expectation, doesn't stop the feeling of being ignored. It's like calling a friend on the phone to share something that you feel is important and them not listening, leaving them a message and them not calling you back.

In truth a celebrity's soul mate and destiny could be lying within no other than that of the fan. A fan could be one of their best friends, someone who could understand them or relate to them like no other, but have never been given the chance. Then of course, rather than giving us that relationship we fantasize about or friendship we dream of, just a response to a genuine letter to say, " I get what your saying," "I feel like that all the time," or just "thank you for your support." The truth is that we are all people.

Even though it is hard for celebrities to really know us or where we are coming from, I think it is important that they know that sometimes we just want a little recognition as individuals. It is sometimes important for us to feel appreciated as fans because of their powerful influence on us. I do believe that there are some fans out there who really want to meet with their idol for all the right reasons.

I have always wondered if celebrities actually do read our letters. I guess I will never know. If so, do they ever come across one that really moves them and do they ever want to meet the person who wrote it? Again, I guess I will never know.

It has been nine months and I am still hoping for a response from *The Ellen DeGeneres Show*. Although I may be waiting a lifetime, facing the reality of a fourth unanswered fan letter, I keep in mind what these stars do for me every day, which is make my life happier and some days easier.

No matter what has been said, I will never be all Clayed out and will probably be singing about being "Invisible" for many days to come. When I am driving in my car with my kids it will always bring a smile to my face when they ask to hear Jason because "Travelin' Thru" sounds like the song from the movie *Curious George*. No matter how good or how bad of a day I am having, it doesn't matter because in the morning I'll be dancing with Ellen. To me, it's like a sweet escape from the frequent obstacles of life which we all know can sometimes be difficult.

These celebrities will always have a special place in my heart because they have all inspired me and have left me with a long lasting influence. So what are my expectations? The truth is, I guess I don't have any. What I expect to happen in life and what I would like to happen in life are two completely different things.

I have always known that the chances of ever getting a response to my letters or meeting my idols and sharing some kind of relationship with them were slim to none. As for what I would like to happen, maybe someday my dreams will come true. Maybe I will meet Clay Aiken or Jason Castro. There may even be a possibility that some day I could be writing about my experience on the *The Ellen DeGeneres Show*.

If you can't dream, there is never hope for what could actually happen.

2007
CD Cover and
Back Cover

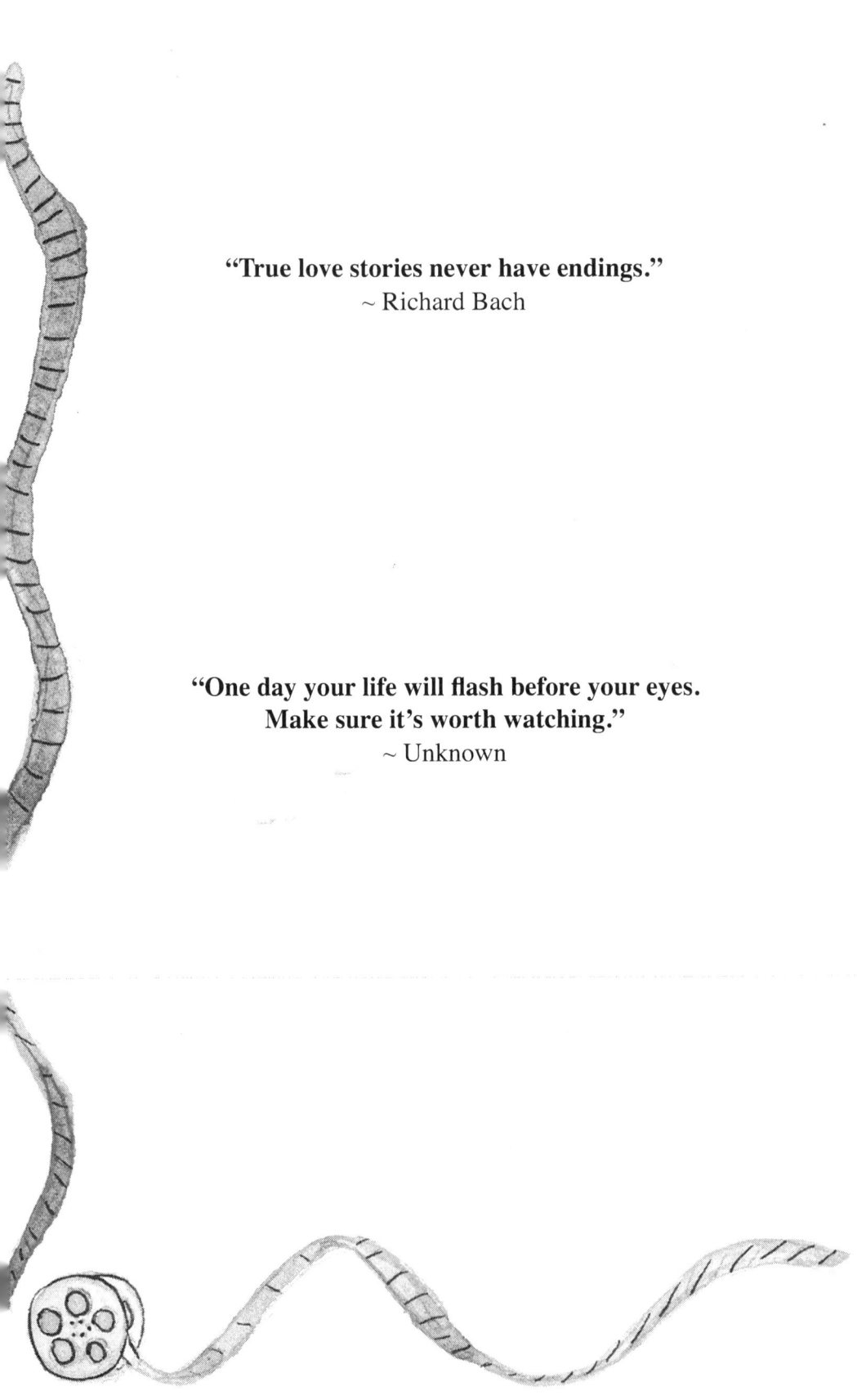

"True love stories never have endings."
~ Richard Bach

"One day your life will flash before your eyes.
Make sure it's worth watching."
~ Unknown

Chapter 14

Almost Famous

As Bryce and I opted to order take out due to lack of food in the house, we decided to try a new Chinese place in town. We just moved into a brand new home and with money being tight, twenty dollars seemed like a lot of money considering the food was absolutely disgusting. I could not even finish what was on my plate so I moved on to the fortune cookie. As I cracked it open, enjoying the only edible thing on the table, my fortune read: Love or money, or neither?

I chose love. Love is what makes the world go 'round, right? Of course it is. For love of my children, to stay home with them from day to day, even if it means sacrificing some of the things that I desire but know that there is always time for those things later in life. It's the now for them and to me, that is important. For love of my husband, who works hard to put a roof over our heads and food on the table and the strength to tolerate my sometimes intolerable hang ups where sometimes I allow fantasy to interfere with reality.

For love of dreaming of what sometimes seems the impossible, but it's sometimes the dream that keeps us going. It is important to keep our dreams alive.

It is November 24th and I just bought the new David Cook CD. While listening to his song "Time Of My Life," I found myself totally engaged as I felt that I could somewhat relate to some of the lyrics through my present experience:

I've been waiting for my dreams

To turn into something

I could believe in

And looking for that

Magic rainbow

On the horizon

I couldn't see it

Until I let go

Gave into love and watched all the bitterness burn

Now I'm coming alive

Body and soul

And feelin' my world start to turn

And I'll taste every moment

And live it out loud

I know this is the time,

This is the time

To be more than a name

Or a face in the crowd

I know this is the time

This is the time of my life

Time of my life

I began to think I felt a connection. I hold my dreams close to my heart, and more than any actual real life experience is the heartfelt experience that I get through the feeling I have when I'm dreaming. I am in some respects living my dream, living it out loud through writing about it, ready to share it with the world. Through writing, I've felt like a weight has been lifted off my shoulders just by being able to express myself, my feelings, and my dreams, as crazy as they may be. More than any encounter, success or celebrity status is feeling alive from the power of dreaming. I will continue to stay grounded but remain open to any opportunity that shall present itself. Should luck come my way, whether it is an actual up close and personal experience or if life stays just the way it is, I truly believe that everything happens for a reason.

There are times in my life when I truly feel that no one fully understands me. There are days that I yearn to just be understood and to be taken seriously. I feel that no one genuinely believes in my ability to someday find what I am looking for, although sometimes I myself am not sure of what that is.

Just recently, Bryce said to me, "You and the kids are my life and I don't know what we would do without you but there is something that is missing from yours, something centering around some kind of fame or success. It's something I cannot give you but something you are going to need to find for yourself or leave me to find someone else who can give you what I can't."

When he said this to me, I actually got a little choked up and teary. There was a piece of me that knew he was right, because even though I do love my husband and my children and I am happy, I do feel at times that something is missing in my life. The only thing he is wrong about is I would never leave my family in order to seek whatever it is that is missing.

Other than my family, I feel that what I am most passionate about is too far out of reach; therefore sometimes I feel that it's not even worth taking the extra steps in seeking it. Frequently, I feel as if I am in this zone. I am all alone in this foggy open room with walls on both sides of me. There is no way around, just fog for miles in front of me and behind. To the right is my husband and children, as the wall is always low enough to climb. To the left, the wall is much too high for me to climb on my own. If I were to get assistance in getting over the top of this wall to experience a journey of the unknown, they may not be able to follow. Therefore, I would never go. I would not even question leaving behind my sole being of happiness for something that I did not even know existed. Even if I knew it did, I could not fully succeed without them and again I would be missing something in my life, something much bigger. Without the unknown, I could survive. Without my family, I could not, for love is the root of everlasting happiness. Nothing is worth exploring if I cannot share it with the people I love most in my life.

I just sat down with some popcorn and soda to watch one of my favorite movies, *Almost Famous*. As I watched the movie many times before, I never realized how relevant it was to answering some of the questions regarding some of the confused feelings that I had been experiencing in my life.

The movie is about a fifteen year old boy named William, who was assigned to write an article for *Rolling Stone* magazine. It evolves into his reflection on the relationship between the two universes, fan and celebrity. As he finds himself amongst a famous rock band, Still Water, he experiences life from a whole different perspective.

He meets Penny Lane, a popular "band aid." When he asks her if she has any regular friends, she responds, "Famous people are more interesting." As Penny discovers that the lifestyles of the rich and famous could not provide her with the one thing that she craved most, love, she returns home to what William refers to as "the real world."

Toward the end of the movie, the jet plane carrying William and the members of Still Water starts to take a dive toward the ground. William reminds them of the importance of the fan. As they were always too caught up in what was superficial, they were too busy to reflect on the more important things in life, love and peoples' feelings.

As the movie comes to a close, one of the groupies speaks about people not understanding what it is like to be a true fan; to love a band or a piece of music so much that it hurts.

As I turned in to bed that night, I thought about the things that were most important in my life. As I closed my eyes feeling happy and content, I again found myself dreaming.

I was almost famous once in a romantic encounter with Jason Castro. I bet you are wondering how that saucy dream ends. Well, it doesn't. It is always open ended, maybe to keep the dream alive, maybe for hope of a dream coming true, or maybe to always make sure that I open my eyes to reality. I have children who need their mother and a husband who needs his wife as much as she needs them, along with the dream.

1995 — AMCAT and me

Bryce and Me — 1996 Senior Ball

1996 Graduation

1998 Graduation

My Family

Ethan 2004

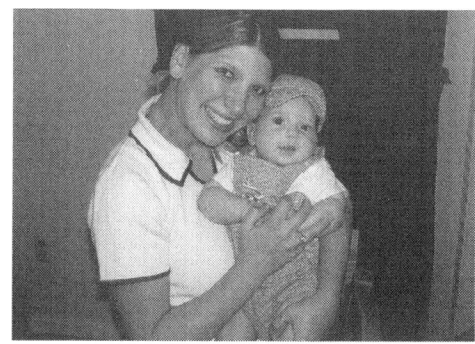

Faith 2007

Ethan and Faith 2010

Christmas 2010

Easter 2011

Spring 2011

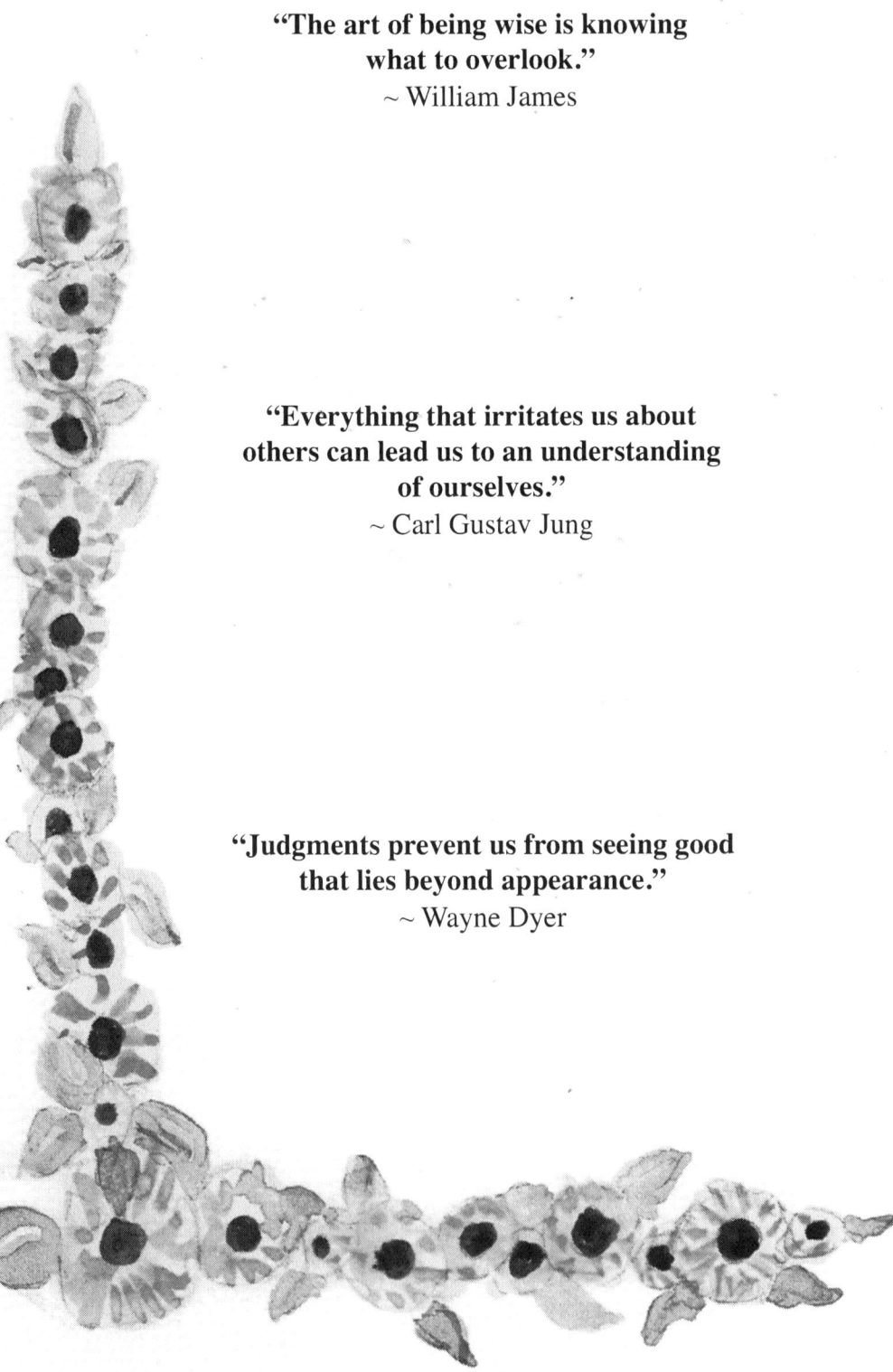

"The art of being wise is knowing
what to overlook."
~ William James

"Everything that irritates us about
others can lead us to an understanding
of ourselves."
~ Carl Gustav Jung

"Judgments prevent us from seeing good
that lies beyond appearance."
~ Wayne Dyer

Chapter 15
Facebook

Although I consider myself to be a pretty level headed person, not going beyond the limits of the obsessive fan, I do tend to go on websites every now and then to get updates on my favorite 'Idols' while waiting for an upcoming CD. In keeping the excitement alive and impatiently waiting for Jason to release his new CD, I was surfing the web looking for any information I could possibly get on new release dates.

While quickly scanning through articles I noticed something on Jason having a girlfriend. I couldn't help but click on it to see what that was all about. There were several posts from fans reactions to the possibility of him having this girlfriend. One woman had commented on them looking cute together and how she was happy for him. Now, correct me if I am wrong, but even though we say that we are happy for them because we want to be and we always mean well, are we really that happy for them? Fans never really want to hear about their favorite celebrity being involved with someone. The truth is, we actually all like to think of ourselves as his or her boyfriend or girlfriend. Sometimes we even refer to them as our boyfriend or girlfriend. Come on my friends, any talk of a significant other just ruins the fantasy for us. Yes, in reality, he is allowed to have a personal life but do we really need to know about it or hear about it for that matter? Just keeping it real, my friends. Just keeping it real.

Anyway, I have always had my reservations about becoming a Facebook member. I decided to join because I was intrigued by this: *"Sign up for Facebook to connect with Jason Castro."*

Although many good experiences such as connecting with old friends, and horrific experiences like the end of my friendship with my former best friend Maria, have come from my Facebook interactions, this was my initial reason for joining. I thought to myself, Could it really be that easy? I seriously doubted it but I was determined to prove a point.

I joined Facebook just shy of getting taken over by a new season of *American Idol*. You got it, season eight. From early auditions, I was already of fan of twenty-nine year old Danny Gokey.

One of my first Facebook interactions was with my sister-in-law, Erica, who asked me if I had been watching (what a silly question), who had referred to having her first "love of her life" Idol crush. At the time, she did not know his name but when she mentioned theater, I remembered his name was Adam.

As I had several friend requests from past friends who had immediately found me, I still needed to research my initial reason for joining Facebook. I typed Jason Castro's name in the search bar and found myself on a page amongst 35,000 other fans and thought that's just what I figured. There was not even an "add as a friend" option but only a "become a fan" option. Furthermore, as I wrote on his wall, remembering that I did not want to overstep that fine line into the irrational fan zone, my post contained only four words, "Is this really you?"

Again, I do not believe that Jason Castro is really reading 35,000 posts and responding to them individually and in reality, how could he? Just like a fan letter he posts a generic message every now and then to 'all' of his fans to update us on his plans and future career. Although it is good to be in the circle of upcoming events, always looking for an opportunity for a Jason fix, there is no true connection or interaction on a personal level. I do enjoy some of the cute videos and of course the "date nights," short videos from wherever Jason is to say hi to his many fans. At least he is making an honest effort in keeping his fan base alive.

I loved reading the posts on my friends' walls every Tuesday and Wednesday night about *Idol* performances and results shows. Either I would smile, laugh or even get a little frustrated about the comments on the most loved and the most hated contestants. I would only find myself chiming in when I agreed or could find humor in a situation, not being a person who likes argument and confrontation.

Facebook also has a cool tool for taking different AI quizzes or even casting votes for your *Idol* favorites. There was always a lot of love for Danny Gokey. One of my friends even once posted that she was going to "fight Paula for her new 'boyfriend' Danny Gokey." There were also many Kris Allen crushes and a lot of very mixed emotions about over the top performances by Adam Lambert.

My friend Bonnie was clearly an Adam Lambert fan. I sent her a message that read, "I'm guessing you are an Adam fan?" I felt like I could really relate to her when she emailed me back and said that "Adam Lambert made her heart flutter." Although I had no real

155

connections or *Idol* crushes this year, I had known from past and even still present experience what it is like to have an *Idol* crush and where it can sometimes take you.

At the end of it all, though, when push came to shove, people started getting downright nasty about the contestants they didn't like as opposed to the ones that they did. There was a lot of sadness after the Danny Gokey elimination and I remember getting really agitated after one post read "Kris Allen is better than Danny Gokey because he plays instruments." There was even more so of an explosion before and after the Adam Lambert vs. Kris Allen finale.

As I was a fan of all of the top three guys, despite musical style, if it was a singing competition and only a singing competition, Adam Lambert should have walked away with the title. Looking at this year's *Idol* from a singing standpoint, I started to get angry with some of the comments like, "Go Kris, kick the screaming drag queen's ass!" and, "Hey Adam, Mary Kay called, she wants her make-up back." I realize that not everybody wants to jump aboard the Adam train when it comes to black nail polish and guy liner, but I was just hoping that wasn't what people were voting on.

Although I would buy a Danny Gokey or Kris Allen CD because I prefer that type of music over rock, I don't believe that it was fair to take away from Adam his amazing vocal ability to sing them all under a table. It showed complete ignorance.

That night my post read, "Congratulations Kris, although when the winner expresses that the title should have gone to his opponent, that is really saying something. It is too bad that society is so caught up in sexual preference. I saw the same thing happen to Clay Aiken 5 years ago." Moments after my post, my Facebook page exploded. I guess you would not think that I am a person who does not like confrontation, but I did not know I was not entitled to my opinion.

I was so fired up that night that I wrote a short article which I tried to submit to several papers including the Worcester Telegram and Gazette, Boston Globe, Boston Herald, Boston Phoenix, Boston Metro, New York Times and Hartford Courant. The article read as follows:

Does Allowing Idol *Contestants to Play Instruments Distract Voters*

"This is a singing competition," a phrase used by Simon Cowell many times in the past. But is Simon mellowing as the years increase?

Presently, in Season Eight of American Idol, *the talented Kristen McNamara was overlooked for having poor choice of attire as the judges filled a wild card vacancy with Meghan Joy who was an embarrassment to the reputation of the show in more ways than one.*

In reality, I think it is fair to say that the general public does not vote purely on vocal talent.

In Season Two, the well known battle of Ruben Studdard and Clay Aiken, Simon commented more than once about America clearly voting on vocal ability seeing as neither one "looked" the part. As many people disagreed with the results of the Season Two Finale, could it have really come down to the publics' choice of what was easier on the eyes, a man who sweat more on stage in five minutes than someone who just ran a marathon or a contestant whom caused redirection for many by his possible sexual preference?

Did Season Three's Fantasia Barrino really have the winning voice or did she just have a better personality than Latoya London?

Was Season Five's Chris Daughtry voted off simply because he was a rocker, or was it because he was lacking in the personality department altogether?

What about power vocalist Carly Smithson? Could it be that too many people were distracted by the mural of a tattoo on her arm to notice that she could deliver instant goosebumps the minute she hit that high note?

Season Seven of American Idol *began a new trend when contestants were allowed to play instruments on the show.*

While discussing American Idol *on a* Facebook *page, I was recently taken by surprise when a friend commented that Kris Allen was better than Danny Gokey because he played two instruments. Is he also a better vocalist than Adam Lambert? Although playing an instrument makes an artist well rounded, does it necessarily make them a better vocalist?*

Would Brooke White, the nanny who won our hearts, have made it to the number five spot on her vocal ability alone? Would Jason Castro, one of my personal favorites, have made it to the number four spot without his acoustic guitar, dreamy eyes and trademark dreads?

In truth, personality does shine through in an artists' ability to play a musical instrument... but is it a personality contest? Could an instrument be a distraction or sometimes compensating for the actual vocal piece?

Voting for an American Idol *contestant is also that of personal preference more than who is actually the best... or maybe people just differ on the idea of what the best is? A lot of fans will cast a vote for their favorites fully knowing that they are not necessarily the best vocalist, but because they prefer a certain type of music and, for example, would not vote for a rocker or an R&B artist no matter how good they are because they would not buy their CD.*

So should they ban contestants from playing musical instruments on the show?

In reality, I don't think it would make a difference. Our society is so distracted by, "lookism", personality (or lack of), and of course the "gay factor", why not add instruments to the mix too....but it is a singing competition....right Simon?

Unfortunately, most of these papers already have writers that cover the entertainment field.

Shortly after the big stir up, I decided to become a fan of more pages on Facebook other than Jason Castro. My pages included Clay Aiken, *The Ellen DeGeneres Show, American Idol, Smallville, The Office* and of course Fenway Park…Go Sox!

The only other post I ever sent Jason Castro was on March 25th which simply stated "Happy Birthday Jason. Take a step back today and relax with family and friends. Surround yourself with the people who matter the most."

Updates on my favorite television shows and celebrities are better than nothing.

"Success is a journey not a destination.
The doing is often more important than
the outcome."
~ Arthur Ashe

"Persistence is the twin sister of excellence.
One is a matter of quality; the other a
matter of time."
~ Unknown

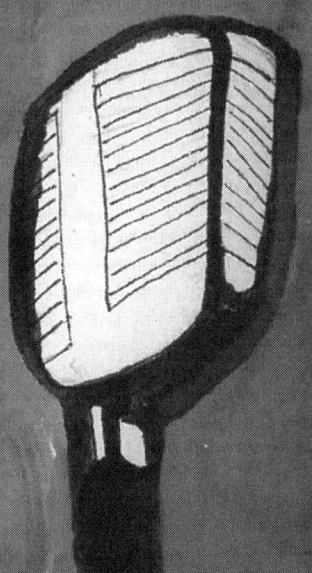

If at first you don't succeed,
get a bigger hammer."
~ Alan Lewis

Chapter 16
If You're Not a Celebrity...Who Cares?

As I once sought after stardom in the past, brought back alive through *American Idol* and its contestants, I began to write about my dreams and passions of singing and relating to these rising stars from this reality show. I figured I am a talented writer, how hard can it be to get a book published if you have both the talent for writing and a great idea?

I began submitting query letters to agents, a couple at a time, in November of 2008. Eight months later, I was lucky to get a lot of positive feedback, but still nobody quite believing in my idea enough to sign me on.

Ironically, one agent had given me hope through an inspiring rejection letter. She had gone on to say that even though that she was passing on my promising work, that persistence leads to success and that every no is closer to a yes. Even though at that point I was discouraged over the number of rejection letters filling my "rejection" folder, luckily, persistence is one of my finer qualities, most of the time. It gave me enough motivation to keep going with it. Soon after that, I got another rejection letter advising me to be more proactive and instead of a proposal stating what I would like to do, to start putting those words into actions. It was at that time that I decided to write another letter to Ellen.

I went to her online site, as I did the first time I sent a letter. Somehow after I had composed what I had wanted to say, it would not let me send it through. I then stumbled onto a website called Verotal Solutions. This was a website with addresses for writing fan letters to your favorite celebrities. I looked up Ellen DeGeneres, Clay Aiken and Paula Abdul in hopes that through letters, one of these stars would hear my voice. As for Jason, I still decided not to send him a fan letter based on my previous Clay heartbreak. My letters read as follows:

Dear Ellen,

I wrote to you in June of 2008 with great hope for a response. Unfortunately, I did not have great luck in connecting with you. Through my letter I was seeking answers to unknown questions regarding celebrity status and fandom and looking to fulfill and keep my dreams alive. I did not find success in a hopeful response but my letter to you and the excitement of awaiting a response led me to follow through with fulfilling another dream, finishing a book that I began writing in 2003.

In my book, Reaching Out to the Stars: American Idol Dreams, *I grapple with the reality of the relationship between celebrities and their fans. This book focuses on my own personal experience of being a fan, many times as a child and now as an adult, my present obsession with the hit reality television show* American Idol *and its popular contestants. My book features my personal fan letters to my "idol obsession" along with my past letter to you in search for reason to why we as fans get so caught up in celebrities of choice, for example, my own guilty pleasure of the* American Idol *experience.*

As I am excited about my work and happy to say that my manuscript is being reviewed by a literary agency, I am hoping that you would support my project as well upon representation and possible publication.

As I have always admired you as my favorite television host, you have also been an inspiration to me, in making the dreams of ordinary people come alive.

Dear Clay,

Although I refuse to call myself a Claymate, I have been a huge fan of yours since 2003. I have sent you three fan letters, this being my fourth. As I never asked for a response, thinking it to be somewhat irrational, a little piece of me was sad when I did not get one.

As I started to grapple with the reality of the relationship between celebrities and their fans, I began to get frustrated. As my mind was filled with unanswered questions, my thoughts began to overflow onto paper. One page developed into a book called Reaching Out to the Stars: American Idol Dreams.

As you were my inspiration for beginning to write this book, I was inspired to finish it after the close of American Idol *(Season Seven) as I became a devoted fan of, yet, another* Idol *contestant.*

I am excited about this project and have been querying agents since November of '08. As I am happy to say that my work is being reviewed by a literary agency, I am hoping that you would support my project as well upon representation and possible publication.

As I have always admired you as my favorite American Idol, *you have been an inspiration to me in more ways than one. I am hoping for your support in putting in a good word, as I know you understand what it is like for an ordinary person to fulfill a dream.*

Dear Paula,

I have been a fan of yours since childhood and have also been a fan of American Idol *since 2003.*

As I have been inspired by this show, I have also been inspired by some of its popular contestants.

As a devoted fan of Clay Aiken, I began to grapple with the reality of the relationship between celebrities and their fans after three unanswered fan letters. As the frustration and mystery of it all consumed me, I began writing a book called Reaching Out to the Stars: American Idol Dreams. *I was able to complete my book upon the close of Season Seven when I was won over by fourth place runner up Jason Castro.*

As I am excited about the completion of this project, I have been looking for representation since November of '08. As I am happy to say that my work is being reviewed by a literary agency, I am hoping that you would support my project as well upon possible representation and publication.

You have always inspired me to follow my dreams as you often inspire the contestants of American Idol. *I was recently told by an agent that persistence leads to success. As I am anxious to fulfill and keep my dreams alive, still I keep reaching out to the stars.*

Again, in hopes for some kind of response, I am still waiting.

With frustration and great persistence, I began to type a new article that I thought I may submit to a local paper.

If You're Not A Celebrity......Who Cares???

American Idol, *Season Seven, Top 24, who am I? I am not a celebrity, but just a fan that experienced a romantic encounter with 4th place runner up Jason Castro…and then I woke up. Haven't we all had that dream before about that one celebrity who makes us a little weak in the knees.*

The truth is, we live in a different world. If you're not a celebrity then who cares! As a child I always dreamed of being famous, as we all probably have at some time in our lives. As I grew older I wondered if that type of lifestyle that we long for was even a happy one. Just lately I finished writing a personal memoir about being a fan and thought, I may not be a star or even want the life of one, but maybe I could be a published author and write about my dreams, my personal obsessions and my passions regarding music.

I then realized, are you kidding me? It is just as hard to become a published author as it is to become a well known star. Why is it that nobody wants to hear the real life stories and experiences inside the world of fandom? After all, without the fan, there would be no star.

I have been querying agents since November. I have had a lot of positive feedback including two requests for my manuscript and still no action. I even had one agent respond to me that "Unless you are famous, memoirs are hard." Now if that doesn't prove my point, then what does?

Once again, I started to become discouraged. Although there were pieces of me that wanted to just give up on my dream, a bigger part of me felt that the more that my voice was not heard, the more persistent I would become on being able to reach for the stars, even though they just may be unreachable. It has never been in my character to give up. Hopefully, that will get me somewhere someday. If you're reading my book, then my persistence paid off.

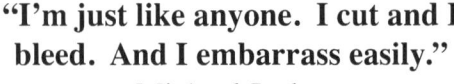

"I'm just like anyone. I cut and I
bleed. And I embarrass easily."
~ Michael Jackson

"Success is to be measured not so much by the
position that one has reached in life as by
the obstacles which he has overcome."
~ Booker T. Washington

"The image is one thing and the human
being is another...It's very hard to live
up to an image, put it that way."
~ Elvis Presley

Chapter 17

A 'King' Is Lost but Never Forgotten

Three months ago, Bryce and I sat watching *American Idol* during Michael Jackson week. As the show began and they showed a clip, our eyes were fixated on the television as we both got goose bumps up and down our spine. As soon as it ended, Bryce and I looked at each other and said, "Do you remember that?"

On June 25th we were celebrating Faith's third birthday. We were sitting on the deck having a cookout with my mom and dad, David and the kids. The kids quickly left the table to play on the swings.

My dad had come from a golf game and said, "Hey, did you hear that Michael Jackson died?" We all looked at each other and laughed as we thought it was another one of my father's far-fetched jokes.

He said, "No, I'm not joking, I'm serious."

I said, "Dad, if that was true it would be all over the media because that would be huge." David actually started yelling at him, as he usually does when he starts to get upset. "That isn't even funny, Dad. You shouldn't even joke about things like that."

I looked up as Bryce returned to the table, not even knowing that he had left, being so caught up in the conversation. As he sat down, he said, "It's true, I just looked it up online." I dropped my fork. I can't even explain the feeling that went through me. I kept saying, "Are you kidding me, are you kidding me?" I could not even eat the rest of my meal. I could tell that David was upset, too. I was not prepared for the huge affect this was going to have on me as a fan and as an individual.

Michael Jackson was a huge part of our childhood. I watched news coverage that night and I was still in shock.

When I woke the next morning, I tuned directly to all of the popular news channels. In five years, I have never started my morning off with anything but PBS Kids. For some reason, I could not tear myself away from the coverage all day.

Memories started flowing through my mind as I watched clips of Michael through the years. I remember like it was yesterday the year Michael Jackson won eleven Grammy awards after *Thriller* was released. The red or blue glittery jacket with the sequined glove and his soft, high pitch voice quickly came to mind. I remember how big the making of *Thriller* was back then.

Finally, I called my mom at work. When she answered the phone, I started to get weepy. She asked me what was wrong. I replied, "I know it sounds crazy but I am so upset about Michael Jackson. I can't stop watching it on television and I keep crying. Is this normal?" She then said in a soothing and understanding voice, "Yes, it is normal. We all did the same thing when Elvis died. Your Michael Jackson is our Elvis."

As I hung up the phone, I felt a little relieved to hear my mom say that it was alright to feel as I was feeling. I then began to play my Michael Jackson CDs and as a tribute to the King of Pop, I danced and sang with my children. I listened to nonstop Michael until it was time to go to bed. It made me feel so much better.

The death of Michael Jackson has made an impact on me in many ways. This terrible tragedy started my endless thinking again. The morning of the 26th of June, as I tuned into *The Today Show*, I remembered Matt Lauer briefly talking with a woman who they immediately cut short. She was bashing Michael Jackson and I remembered her saying that Michael was obsessed with fame. Matt Lauer quickly shot back at her with the words, "Was he obsessed with it or was he a victim of it?"

Thinking back on that interview, I was a bit angry.

We as children grow up with idols like Michael Jackson. We look up to them, want to be like them and we cherish the art of the music they bring into our lives that we will never forget. They become a part of us. Artists such as MJ are born with a God given talent that gives us the joy of being able to know it and love it. We think that being famous is a great thing and as children and even as adults, sometimes we don't understand it.

Even though Michael loved being a performer, that is all he knew about life. He did not have a choice. He would never know what it is to have a normal life any more than most of us will know what it is like to walk a day in his shoes. Sometimes I feel like someone of his legacy almost makes a sacrifice to deliver an incredible artistry to all mankind.

We have normal everyday lives and even though we all think that dream, we can somehow live it through them. In a reverse situation, sometimes I think that Michael's other passion was to help children to appreciate their childhood, as he never had a normal one of his own. Unfortunately, labeled as strange, it's too bad that a lot of people forget about all the good he did as a human being along with his talent just because of false accusations that some people chose to believe.

Maybe experiencing the life of a fan, we would like to keep our normalcy but be a little more like them. Maybe they would like to continue their careers as artists and to be a little more like us, unless wanting what we can't have is just part of being human.

With regard to a life of fame as opposed to a life of normalcy, I think I should start to be more thankful for what I have. At least when I am sporting a headset while playing Karaoke Play Station and drooling over my favorite *Idol* contestant, the only ones who can label me as strange are my family and friends. I'm not a celebrity and I don't care.

Michael Jackson has left an imprint in my heart forever, not only as a legendary artist, but also as a human being.

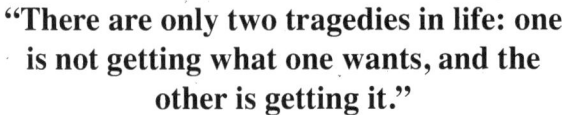

**"There are only two tragedies in life: one
is not getting what one wants, and the
other is getting it."**
~ Oscar Wilde

**"I would rather be able to appreciate
things I can not have than to have things
I am not able to appreciate."**
~ Elbert Hubbard

Chapter 18
Mohegan Sun

It is July 30th, 2009 and I can't believe that Bryce and I are going to be celebrating our tenth Anniversary. As we never get away with the kids, we originally had thought for our tenth that we would go back to New York City. Laney had even offered to hook us up with an awesome place. We had been looking forward to it. The only problem was, we should have known from the get go that it was not going to happen.

We have children who do not sleep! Therefore, nobody was jumping off the edge of their seats to take them for an overnight. We had pretty much given up when my friend Katie had offered to stay with the kids here at the house with her two kids. Katie and I met a year ago when Ethan started preschool at age three. Her son, John, and Ethan were in the same class.

Ethan was definitely suffering from some major separation anxiety. I don't know who took it worse, Ethan or me. So far, one of the hardest experiences for me as a mother was my son crying, "Mommy don't go" and having to turn my back and walk away from him. I'm not sure who cried harder. So when the year ended, Katie called me over the summer to get the boys together. They ended up being friends and so did we. She also had a daughter, Avery, who was only a year younger than Faith.

I was unsure at first whether to take her up on her offer. I had nothing but complete trust but did not want to leave her with a possible nightmare. As New York seemed a little far for us to be away from the kids, in case we were needed back home, we settled for a night at Mohegan Sun which was only one hour away. Although it was not New York, it was a lot of fun.

When we said goodbye to the kids, they seemed excited about their sleepover. I had bought them new sleeping bags and tried to talk it up a lot. As I knew I would miss them, I was also looking forward to a night amongst adults.

As we entered into the valet parking lot at the casino, the attendant took our car and we entered the hotel lobby. I had been to Mohegan only two other times, Clay Aiken and Clay Aiken. I was admiring the atmosphere like it was my first time there, and my heart started to grow with excitement.

We made our way to the check in counter and got the keys to our room, on the seventh floor. We had never stayed overnight so we were not really sure what to expect. As we got into the elevator, I held on to Bryce as if I was jumping out of a helicopter. Anyone who knows me well would probably be surprised that I did not walk up seven flights of stairs. I again recalled when we took our trip to New York City. Uncle Tony teased me about my fear of elevators. Each time we entered and exited our hotel, I would turn as white as a sheet.

The elevator doors finally opened on the seventh floor, which was in seconds that felt like hours, and we made our way down to our room. As we entered, we saw a small living area and thought, where do we sleep? We looked further and saw there was a bedroom that was separate off the living area with a walk in closet containing a safe and his and her bathrobes. Then we made our way to this amazing bathroom.

Looking straight into the bathroom from the doorway was a huge glass shower stall, the toilet tucked in its own private area to the left of the stall. Upon entering, on the right was a double sink vanity and on the left a jetted tub with a full paned, one way view window overlooking the casino.

When I looked at Bryce with my jaw dropped to the floor, it was like looking into a mirror because he looked the same way. I could not help but feel somewhat important, and then I thought, *is this how they live times one million?* It then, at that moment, hit me like a ton of bricks.

I think I felt I had a glimpse into the life of a star for a second. Even though I am not a celebrity, having a little more than I was used to, it was all relevant. With how excited and happy I felt at that moment, I started to think that maybe just having a little more than we are used to every once in awhile was all it took. There was no need for a life of stardom. As a matter of fact, having the most you could possibly have everyday in your life would probably get boring after awhile and then to what would you have to look forward? I think sometimes we lose appreciation for things when we get too spoiled. Maybe that is why it is also best to keep our favorite celebrities at an arm's length and to be careful for what we wished.

That night we won five hundred bucks on a slot machine. Bryce is the one who won it which was weird because I am usually the lucky one. He said he did not understand because he never wins anything, as he wore a smile from ear to ear. Then I noticed that he was also wearing Uncle Tony's ring. I know that Uncle Tony was sitting on his shoulder that night. With that money, we paid for the repairs on our Chevy Blazer, the car that Aunt Carol and Uncle Tony had given us. Maybe he knew we needed a little help at that moment.

We enjoyed ourselves that night, not turning in to bed until 2 a.m. I was a little worried about being too tired when we got home the next day where the great every day responsibilities awaited us. We drove home in buckets of rain and picked up the kids at Katie's house. Faith greeted us with a smile but Ethan clearly had missed us as he got very emotional when we walked in. I think he was angry at us for leaving. He kept crying on the way home.

Our next adventure out would be in a couple of weeks to see *American Idols Live, Season Eight*, in Boston on August 18th. Although it would not be an overnight, I knew Ethan would not be pleased. I thought it may just be best to leave the kids with my parents as we mostly did on the rare occasions when we would actually go somewhere. That is where the kids are most comfortable and that is who I am most comfortable leaving them with.

"Twenty years from now you will be more disappointed by the things that you didn't do than by the ones that you did do. So throw off the bowlines. Catch the trade winds in your sails. Explore. Dream. Discover."
~ Mark Twain

"Your life is an occasion. Rise to it."
~ Suzanne Weyne

"A lot of people are afraid to say what they want. That's why they don't get what they want."
~ Madonna

"Never tell me the sky is the limit when there are footprints on the moon."
~ Unknown

Chapter 19
Life Is What You Make It

August 19, the day after another *American Idol* adventure, and I was off to record a new song at my brother's house. David had agreed to let me record another song as long as I used my own karaoke music and he did not have to create any of the music for me. I had just found out prior to leaving home that Jason Castro was releasing a single from his new album that was still in the works.

I drove and listened to "Light On" by David Cook, trying to learn the song that I was going to be recording in forty minutes. I also kept rewinding the night of the show in my head. It was like another experience that I was trying to keep alive through constant thought because I never wanted it to end.

Bryce got home early the night of the concert so that I could shower and get ready for the show. He walked in the door at 3:30 and we were supposed to leave for Boston at 4:30. It did not quite work out as we planned.

My parents were supposed to be over the house for 4:30 but got held up at the hospital where my dad was having a follow up appointment for his fractured shoulder which he got in a motorcycle accident in the beginning of July. The doctor was running three hours behind and they had called to say they would be late. At 4:35, I started to panic. I was getting anxious because I knew that if we did not leave by five we would miss the beginning of the show. After paying a large sum of money to get phenomenal seats, I really did not want to be late.

I started to think about who the first two contestants were to be eliminated this season, who we would most likely miss. I was not concerned at all about missing Megan Joy but I did like Michael Sarver. Therefore, my goal was to get there on time. We had planned to eat before the show but then I thought, *If we get there in time we could catch Michael and go eat while the horrific caw-calling girl performed.*

I had called my neighbor to see if there was any way she could come over with the kids until my parents arrived. As she too was on her way home, she said that she thought she would be able to get here to save us a little time. She showed up around 5:10 and we kissed the kids goodbye and hurried on our way.

We began our drive to the Boston Garden, I was anxious to get there. I was really stressed out because I was in charge of reading the directions, and when you're the directions manager on a trip to Boston, you need to be quick because anyone knows that if you miss a turn in Boston, holy shit, you are screwed.

In college, I remember riding with my friend Jake in the Anna Maria College van to the Boston Art Museum for a field trip for our religion class senior year. We ended up taking a wrong turn and we were so lost that we didn't get there until the tour was three quarters over.

Forgive me my fellow Bostonians, but I have only been to New York City once in my life and could probably figure out my way there better than in my own capital city. There are seven million exits, all close together, tunnels everywhere surrounded by seven million one way streets and somehow, none of them are connected. It has to be the most confusing city ever and it is scary shit.

I managed to get us to the Government Center garage in one piece. When we parked and walked out of the garage, Bryce and I looked at each other at the same time after looking around and had no clue where the Boston Garden even was. Flipping up the cell phone, the time read 6:48. We tried to ask the garage attendant directions but 'no speaka da englas.' I spotted some woman with a glittery *American Idol* t-shirt and as I grabbed Bryce I said softly, "Follow that woman…she knows the way."

We finally made our way to our section. I got excited when I saw the souvenir booth but was bummed out that it would have to wait until later. I placed my foot on the top stair to make our way down to our seats. The arena went black and the music started as you were listening to the introduction to the actual television show on Tuesday night. The timing was impeccable and we made it!

Sitting in our fabulous seats, all of ten feet from the stage, the music was still playing and I got a rush through my body. I leaned over to Bryce and said, "Can you actually picture what it would be like sitting on the set of this show as they are filming?"

Michael Sarver was the first to perform. The two things that I remember about him most was his friendliness to the crowd and a single comment that he made to the fans. "Is there someone here who you love tonight?" The entire place erupted and I thought, *it's not me this year*. Although that connection was absent, I had a great fondness for at least four of them whom I was very excited to see perform.

As Meghan Joy entered with a hot pink number and shoes higher than Mount Washington, I could not deny her beauty. However, she had absolutely no stage presence and could not walk in the shoes. I could not even bring myself to clap for her.

I feel bad for being so anti-Meghan, but I can't seem to get by her erratic behavior on the show. I saw an interview after she was eliminated and she still wasn't getting it. The judges were not upset with her comment regarding not caring about what Simon had said. It was her complete attitude about the elimination and how she almost made a joke of it with her funny faces and so on. Most contestants are very nervous and serious on the elimination show because they do not want to go home. It is an opportunity for a career that most are hoping for, the mere reason for trying out for the show to begin with. It was like she made a mockery of it. Maybe it was the only way that Meghan knew how to deal with the rejection. Unfortunately, it showed her immaturity, it was not good for the show and it turned off viewers. It would not be surprising to me if it even had an effect on her fellow contestants. She was basically making a joke of an opportunity from which they were all hoping to make a career.

Performances by Anoop "Dogg" Desai and Lil Rounds were both solid along with Scott Macintyre who was a bit outshined by Matt Giraud, a definite showman on stage. As he was singing "Hard to Handle," he owned that piano on his feet. It was quite impressive but my first thought was, *Top Gun*, Maverick and Goose, and "Great Balls of Fire."

During the intermission Bryce went to the men's room and told me to get in line for food. As I turned and spotted the souvenirs once again, I thought to myself, *but honey, there is nobody in that line right now. I must take the path less traveled by the hungry because the program and the t-shirt were much more important than eating at that very moment.* I also bought an 8 x 10 of Adam Lambert for my friend Bonnie.

After inhaling a hot dog, we returned to our seats for the top four, and my four favorites. As I was somewhat partial to Danny Gokey, I enjoyed Allison and Kris and was just purely excited to see a live performance by Adam.

One of my favorite examples of an 'idol crush' all night was what I saw when Allison Iraheta took the stage. There was a little boy about three rows down from us who had to be about thirteen years old. He was trying desperately to get her attention. He had purchased her 8x10 photo at the souvenir booth and was holding it up every moment she was on stage. The poor little man's arms must have been ready to fall off by the time he put it down. I felt so bad for him because he just wanted her to notice him. A simple wave probably would have made his night. In fairness to Allison, she was concentrating on her performance and she probably couldn't see past a certain point with the lighting.

Allison had a great performance. My favorite was "Cry Baby," which I was hoping she would perform because it was one of my favorite performances by her on the show. I downloaded that song on iTunes and I listen to it all the time. Before her last song, she got the crowd prepared for Danny, Adam and Kris. The room erupted and no doubt about it, everyone was awaiting the performances of all three. They were definitely the most loved trio of the season.

As the music blared and a loud voice said, "Number three, Danny Gokey", the room again exploded with screams and applause. Danny was my favorite all season. I always seemed to think that he had a little bit of a Robert Downey, Jr. thing going on. I do still believe that the title should have gone to Adam. I think it should have been Kris at three, Danny at two and Adam at number one. Oh well, it is what it is.

Danny came on stage wearing a black jacket over a red button down shirt with jeans, sporting black boots and of course, a different pair of glasses, which became his trademark. Halfway through his set, he dropped the jacket exposing the red button down short sleeved fitted shirt which drew my attention to his arms, which was something I never had noticed before. Holy crap, Danny Gokey was buff. I have to say that was a complete turn on for me. What was ironic is I never really notice things like that, but oh, I did.

Out of all the contestants, Danny was the one who interacted the most with the fans. He actually had a message as he reminded us that the death of his wife had set him forth on this journey which was a blessing for him. He said, "Bad things are going to happen, but don't let your dreams die." He was very inspiring.

As Danny finished his set he formed his arms in the shape of a heart as he did the many times on the show. I wish I could have gotten a picture of that but it was so quick that I missed the opportunity.

The most exhilarating part of the night was when it was Adam's turn to come on stage. Adam's presence provoked excitement for everyone because people were envisioning what his performance would be like.

"Number two, Adam Lambert." The crowd was on their feet. Adam opened with, "Whole Lotta Love" and it was like someone hit the rewind button and I was experiencing the eighties all over again. The black leather suit, the smoke and the voice that went completely through you was something that I have never heard nor experienced in my entire life. Adam was in a league of his own, as Simon Cowell had said many times on the show.

Midway through his set, while performing "Mad World," I looked around at the thousands of people holding up their cell phones in place of lighters which pointed out a definite change in the times for me personally. After his duet with Allison, "Slow Ride," he too shed his coat. I was not sure what was going on that night with the guys and the stripping but there must have been something in the air or maybe the water.

Adam was just a born performer. As his dance moves started to get a little bit suggestive I thought to myself, "Keep it PG Adam, keep it PG." Actually I noticed that Bryce seemed a little uncomfortable with it and I started to laugh.

"Number one, Kris Allen." I screamed for Kris. I did not do that for anyone else. I almost felt like the audience needed to be supportive because how the hell can anyone follow Adam Lambert? Kris did the right thing in switching his instruments from acoustic guitar to piano to electric guitar and back to acoustic. He proved that he was a well rounded musician with a great voice with his own unique style. That is all he needed to do.

Kris closed with "Hey Jude," which I loved because I too am a Beatles fan. As the whole group joined in they ended with "Don't Stop Believin'."

Great show, but I found that at the end the only thing I could think about was Danny Gokey's arms. Exiting the show, I think I actually left with a little Gokey crush and a little disappointed that I had not bought the 8 x 10 for myself which I came close to buying.

My excitability over Danny's arms has become the newest thing for Bryce and I to joke about at home. As a matter of fact, I just recently sent him an email at work saying that I was having a hard time getting the cap off of a bottle of apple juice for the kids and was wondering if he could come home and 'Gokey' it open.

Now that the show had sadly come to an end, all we had to do was get out of Boston. Good luck! I wasn't actually comfortable until we hit the last toll and heard, "Welcome to Woosta, that'll be a dolla twenty five." We came home to sleeping babies who had a good time with their gramma and papa. I was excited but ready to get some sleep so that I could post my pictures and read my program the next day.

As I went to bed that night, I started to reflect on my experiences through life…my hopes, my dreams, my fears and the importance of life as it is as opposed to what we would like it to be. I thought about the dreams that I had laid to rest along with the dreams that I still have alive within me.

I think of the times where I can just sit in a room with my husband and we are able to spend time with each other even if sometimes we never have a thing to say. I think about the sound of laughter when my children are playing and the times that there is just nothing to do and that's alright. I thanked God for the simple life that we sometimes take for granted but also for the uplifts such as a simple trip to Mohegan Sun to get away for a night or an *American Idol* adventure.

I also thought of the lives of the present idols. As I read my program, I took great interest in the letters to the fans. These letters made me realize that this show that I had come to love so much along with its contestants does not only inspire its viewers and followers, but also inspires its contestants themselves who are actually somewhat inspired by us fans.

Addressed as fans or even friends, which made perfect sense to me, I hung on to the inspiring words best said by Danny Gokey:

"This time on *American Idol* has brought so much new hope back into my life. It has allowed me to reach out once again towards my dreams in a time where all my dreams seemed to have been shattered. I hope that my journey on *American Idol* has helped you or inspired you to follow your hearts aspirations no matter what obstacles stand in front of you. Sometimes it can be hard work or even painful at times but in the end you'll find out that it was worth all your efforts."

I could not help myself.

Dear Danny,

Writing a fan letter and wondering if the person you are writing to will actually get it, read it and understand it, is a dream within itself...but through inspiration, it is worth a try.

I am 35 years young and happily married with two beautiful children. As I once dreamed of a career as a vocalist, I gave up the dream for a career I felt was more promising, a guidance counselor (now a stay at home mom).

Although it seemed a struggle, I finally felt that even though I am passionate about singing, it was not the life for me considering I don't always like being in the limelight and that I have a family.

I have been inspired by American Idol *since season two because I think it has been easier to live my dream through people like you.*

You have inspired me through your strength in dealing with overcoming obstacles in your own life as well as the American Idol *journey.*

There are days that I still feel like something is missing in my life, which sometimes I cannot even understand. In pursuing my own

American Idol *dreams without the actual experience that you have lived, I began to write a book in 2003 about being a fan of* American Idol *and its contestants.*

In the long and discouraging process of representation and publication, lately I keep your message in mind about keeping my dreams alive. I am hoping to have success with this book, not for money but for excitement and personal accomplishment. Although my voice has not yet been heard, I hope that my writing will lead to a second book on my selected idol favorites and how the American Idol *journey and afterlife has affected them.*

One day I hope to personally spend a day with Danny Gokey. You have been an inspiration to me and many others. I wish you the best of luck with your musical career, your ongoing courage in dealing with the loss of your wife and the hope that you will find that kind of love again sometime in your future.

Weeks later, I received a signed eight by ten of Danny Gokey, not by Danny himself, but from my friend Jodi who knew I was upset about not getting one at the show. Jodi has always been a great friend to me and has always accepted my quirkiness as an enjoyable quality.

What it all comes down to is, life is what you make of it. Whether you are trying to become a star, meet a star, or writing a book, or achieving the goals that you always wanted to reach, "Failure is not an option" as spoken by Michael Sarver.

I think there is a point in everyone's life where there is that something which begins the realization of the reality of their dreams, whether it's a book, a specific individual, a television show, et cetera. It's all in the steps we take to follow those dreams through.

Then I thought to myself, *what happens when there is no more American Idol?* Although that will be a very sad day for me, I believe that when someone is as inspired as I have been by the television show *American Idol* and it's contestants, it is easier to be motivated to seek new inspirations in the future.

I think that throughout life everybody will have their Clay Aiken, who will someday be replaced with a Jason Castro or a Danny Gokey and so on. Maybe my inspiration to be a star leading to my inspiration to meet a star has now inspired me to accomplish the goal I have had to be an aspiring author. In time, maybe new inspirations will lead to new works of art.

2009
American Idols Live Tour
TD Bank North Garden, Boston MA

Kris Allen

Adam Lambert

Allison Iraheta

2009
American Idols Live Tour
TD Bank North Garden, Boston MA

Matt Giraud & Scott Macintyre

Matt Giraud

Danny Gokey

2009
American Idols Live Tour
TD Bank North Garden, Boston MA

Lil Rounds

Anoop Desai

Season 8 Top 11

"Some desire is necessary to keep life
in motion."
~ Unknown

"Keep your heart open to dreams. For as
long as there's a dream, there is hope, and as
long as there is hope, there is joy in living."
~ Anonymous

"Success is not the key to happiness. Happiness is
the key to success. If you love what you are doing,
you will be successful."
~ Albert Schweitzer

"The living moment is everything."
~ D.H. Lawrence

"Yesterday is history. Tomorrow is a mystery.
Today is a gift. That's why we call it
the present."
~ Babatunde Olatunji

Chapter 20

Berklee's Café 939 (Live at the Red Room)

American Idol began its ninth season. Somewhere in between my favorite television host, Ellen, joining the panel of judges, my immediate appreciation for the talented Crystal Bowersox and my tiny attraction to the crooked smile of Lee Dewyze, was a performance which supplied me with the knowledge of an upcoming show featuring the reunion of Rueben and Clay.

As I quickly hit the computer and logged on to Ticketmaster, I found that they were still working on an upcoming tour schedule.

Although still a huge Clay fan and an ongoing fan of *American Idol*, fearing its retirement at the end of the season, life for the last couple of years has been nothing but Castromania. While I was still on the Ticketmaster site, I typed in the magic words "Jason Castro" and found to my surprise that he would be performing at Berklee's Café 939, live at the Red Room. I immediately asked Bryce if he would take me. Of course, it was a go and I immediately ordered two tickets for this May 15th performance in Boston. I was extremely excited for this event but had also found that in these present days of idol craze and other every day events in my life that I was incredibly stressed out.

Without realizing it at the time, for a long time things that normally were hobbies in my life that I enjoyed, things that would typically make me happy, I somehow found a way to make them stressful. For example, scrapbooking had changed from a joyful and happy event to an "Oh my God I have so much to do in these albums and no time to do it." Martial arts had taken a back seat to book submission deadlines and to top it off I ended up sick three weeks before the show, which I was also somehow stressing out about. I had not been sleeping and I had totally lost my voice due to a virus and complete exhaustion. Even though I always had my music as my very first source of relaxation, usually Jason Castro tunes, I was frustrated that I could not even sing to them.

The night of May 8th, Bryce's 36th birthday, my friend Jodi was up from Maine to visit because she was home to spend Mothers' Day weekend with her family. We had started to talk about what was going on in our lives and I began to realize that I had been in denial about the amount of stress that I had been allowing to take over my body and how unhealthy it was.

I began telling her how excited I was about the show but even how much more stressed out I had become about it from not having a thing to wear, still carrying an extra 10 pounds, to the possibility that I could meet Jason due to the small venue he was playing in.

All this time it had been my dream to meet one of my *American Idol* crushes and now that I had this opportunity, I was not sure I wanted it. I always pictured myself meeting one of them and sitting and having a conversation with them person to person never wanting them to perceive me as the ordinary fan but someone they could be friends with. It seemed too overwhelming. I also was sick and worried about feeling nasty in the busy city, no quick way home to where I am so accustomed to being nowadays.

Jodi had been taking classes to be a life coach and was talking to me about my stress and felt that I really needed to take a step back and try to enjoy just the smallest things in life, such as a cup of coffee, not just sucking it down in the morning as I usually do, but taking a moment to actually enjoy it. She sent me an email of links, momentary sensory experiences that link us to joy, feelings of peace, safety, delight, connection and abundance. This is when I decided I needed to take her advice and pause to fully take in the things that inspire and relax me.

A couple of days before the big event, I really started to rest and relax so that I could feel good enough to go to this show which I knew would be inspiring within itself. As I started to put together something to wear, I had come to a pretty quick decision that I was not going to make a big deal about it. I wanted to be comfortable so I decided to just dress comfortable, as I have always felt that less is more.

I woke up the morning of the concert and tried not to think a lot about it until it was time to get ready to go. I was immediately dreading the ride into Boston and found myself a bucket of nerves the minute we pulled out of the driveway. I put on my Jason CD and tried to close my eyes and put my head back and relax.

Of course, after taking the Copley exit, we got lost. Feeling like I was going to either puke or have a major anxiety attack, I quickly texted David "Lost in Boston...Help." He called me almost immediately. As he talked us to Boylston Street, we immediately

201

parked in the Boston Common Garage, no more fooling around. I knew it was too good to be true when we found a space right away because as we walked through the Common to Boylston Street, as I looked up at number 120 I looked at Bryce and said, "We need to walk to 939?"

It took us thirty minutes to reach The Red Room and the line was already backed up about ten feet, an hour and a half before the show. As a woman began to give us an update on what was going on behind the scenes, she informed us that they would open the doors after the sound check and there was no seating, standing room only on a first come first serve basis. As I was already trying to fan myself with my tickets, I looked at Bryce and said, "I am not sure this is worth it. I am too old for this shit." He immediately said with surprise, "Jason is not worth the wait?" I told him I would let him know after the show.

The doors opened at 7:45 and we ended up standing in the second row by the left wall which had an opening like a window you could look out of to the hallway along the side of the small room. We were so close to the stage. I remember thinking that I could have rolled up a napkin and hit him in the head with it.

The opening act was Michael Castro, Jason's brother. Knowing that he tried out for *American Idol* twice and did not make the cut, after watching him perform I wondered what *American Idol* was thinking. He was really good. He had a great voice, played both guitar and piano and had a really good sense of humor. He was also a very talented songwriter.

At 8:30, the second opening act began, Camera Can't Lie. As I could feel the music vibrating through my body, it was a little too loud for my taste. By the time they finished, I was just hoping that I could still hear when it was Jason's turn to hit the stage. Bryce liked them. They dedicated a song to Red Sox fans which was cool and some jackass started yelling some crap about loving the Yankee's. Only an asshole would do that in Boston. I just don't get it.

I remembered when they were about half way through, I caught a glimpse of Jason walking to the left of me to the men's room. As I turned in surprise to catch a quick glimpse of him there was a guy behind me who saw the excitement in my eyes and started laughing. Then he said to me, "Don't be a stalker." When I could not help but keep looking over my shoulder, Bryce shook his head smiling and said, "He is going to be standing five feet from you in about five minutes".

Finally as 9:30 rolled around, it was Jason's turn. I believe I had waited long enough. As he came on stage, it seemed a little surreal. I was so close to him it was crazy.

He was wearing a black t-shirt with light blue torn jeans with an acoustic guitar around his neck. He wore two gold chains, one holding a cross. He had several bracelets on his wrist and his hair was crazy. I turned my camera on to take pictures throughout the show but did not refrain from taking it all in because I really wanted to enjoy the moment. Jodi would have been proud of me.

He sometimes spoke in between songs. Although he seemed comfortable performing in front of the small crowd, it was obvious to me that he still had an uneasiness about him when he spoke. It was like he portrayed this goofy charm as a defense mechanism to deal with the interaction with the fans. Jason was great. He sounded just as good live as he does recorded. He did an unplugged version of "Hallelujah" right before his encore which was amazing. He then announced that he would be in the back hanging out after the show. That is when I was slapped with the huge reality that I may actually meet Jason Castro.

As we started to leave the room, the stage now empty, it was nearing eleven o'clock. We had told the sitter we would be home around midnight. I turned to Bryce and said, "We can wait, right?"

He actually made it pretty clear that we needed to go because we needed to be home by twelve and there was no telling how long we would be waiting. As I turned facing the room we had just exited, Jason was walking right toward me. As I could not take my eyes off of him, he never looked up from the floor passing right by me and headed toward the table in the back of the small room with Michael and Camera Can't Lie.

He was now about ten feet away from me, a pool of excited fans separating us. I began to grow really sad because I knew this was an opportunity that I did not want to let pass me by. I had waited a lifetime for this opportunity and at that moment it was all about Jason.

I looked at Bryce and said, "If you think that I came here to stand on my feet for five hours and leave here without getting a picture with him when he is standing ten feet away from me, you are f'in crazy."

As I started forward, I looked back at him and said, "You're coming with me because you need to take the picture so let's go." He was not happy with me, to say the least, but I did not care. While waiting amongst the crowd, Bryce bought two CD's from the lead singer of Camera Can't Lie. I really wanted Michael's alb, his reference to his EP as a short album, but time was an issue so I decided I would catch up with him on iTunes. As I kept pushing my way through, within ten minutes I was the next to see Jason.

I was anxious, but I patiently waited for the fifty-something year old women and her two teenage daughters to have their time with him. The woman had handed her phone to Jason, as I overheard that one of the daughters could not be there. Then I was thinking to myself, "Oh my God, now I have to wait for him to finish a phone conversation." After he finished the conversation, she kept going on about how much she loved him and how she loved him on Facebook and as he seemed a little uncomfortable, he was really patient and polite. She finally started to move away but got stuck in the crowd and I could not make my way to him as he was just kind of wedged in the corner.

Although up to that point I never made eye contact with Jason, I was amazed at how aware he was about what was going on around him. He definitely saw me waiting to get to him as he wedged his way behind the woman and stood directly in front of me, arms open as to say "Alright, here I am, I got around her." As he made eye contact with me for a quick moment, he started to laugh about the situation and I also started laughing. At that moment, I was looking right at his face and as he kind of crouched down to my level, I realized that he was not that much taller than me. I always felt hugely attracted to Jason but there are no words to describe how I was feeling at that moment looking right into his beautiful face. It was amazing.

As we both stood their laughing, I could not speak a word to him. I almost wanted to say, "I guess I am as bad at this as you are." What could I really have said to him without sounding as stupid as the woman in front of me sounded? Artists know you love them. That's why we are there to watch them.

As Jason saw Bryce standing there with the camera, he just kind of knew that I wanted a picture with him so there was no need to ask. As I stood beside him and put my arm around his waist, all I felt were dreads. I believe I started to shake a little as he put his arm around me for the picture.

After Bryce took the picture and started to lower the camera I said, "Take another one." I then heard the next girl in line who was waiting patiently as I just was say, "That is a good idea."

After the second picture, I let go of him and turned to him but again I was lost for words. He just looked at me and folded his arms awkwardly and he said something, but I am not really sure what he said as I was still somewhat overwhelmed as to what was actually going on. I just had my arm around Jason Castro! As I walked away from him and left with Bryce my heart was racing and I was so excited to see my picture with him, the one and only memory that I would have of that night forever other than what would remain in my head for weeks to come. Just to be clear, it was definitely worth the wait!

As we walked quickly down Boylston Street to get to our car I was trying not to pee myself because I had to go so badly. I was trying to keep my mind off of how badly I needed to go by reflecting on this experience I had just encountered.

We reached the parking garage and got into our car, and not long after exiting the garage we got lost again. Why Boston, why? As we finally found the Mass Pike entrance, I called Kendra, the sitter, to tell her that we would be home closer to one in the morning.

Sleeping that night was difficult. I kept replaying in my mind the events that took place that night, and actually meeting Jason Castro. It had all happened so quickly and I could only get it back through memory. I kept thinking about the fact that I did not let it all in when it was happening, just like the coffee. Sorry Jodi.

As it kept replaying in my mind, sometimes to song, I felt like I was in an episode of *Glee*. Not only do I love that show for the music and for the singing, but it is just the fact that we all at one time in our lives or more take a situation and replay it as a production in our minds. The show is so close to real as far as where our imagination wants to take us…to some musical fantasy.

I had to wait until Sunday night to develop my pictures because the day after the show, my in-laws were coming to celebrate Ethan's sixth birthday. After the small party, as Bryce put the kids into the bath, I went to CVS and waited for my pictures to be developed. I did get my picture of Jason and I in an 8 x 10, which is now sitting framed on my nightstand.

Even though I could not take it all in at the moment it happened, I am thoroughly enjoying the experience to its fullest from what remains in my mind from that night.

As I recapped it to Jodi via phone conversation after she saw my cherished picture on Facebook, was the experience all I expected it to be? The answer to that question is twofold, yes and no.

When I first started thinking about my interaction with Jason, I was beating myself up about it. For so long you dream about a moment like this and when it comes right down to this dream coming true, it never quite ends up like you hoped it would. I was mad at myself for not saying anything to him. I was mad at myself that I did not even thank him for the picture. On a good note, he will never remember that. I was mad that I did not soak up every moment of what was going on when it was happening. Then I thought, *why didn't I at least ask him for a hug?* Then I would have been able to answer my own question of what he smelled like!

I even started to think about all of the fan letters I had written. As Jason was the one and only person I never sent a fan letter to out of fear, I started to think maybe he would have been the most reachable out of any of them. I continued to overanalyze it, realizing that I did things just fine. My interaction with him was probably better than anything I could have dreamed about. Sometimes you don't need to say anything. Words can be read into, picked apart, and at least I didn't say anything stupid to him that I regretted afterwards. I think our mutual laughing together was better than anything I could have hoped for, an experience not ruined by words. I always thought of Jason as someone I could laugh with, and he was.

When I started writing my book, I was confused and curious about the meaning of a life of fame. I always had this goal to meet one of my idols, which I now had.

Bryce will probably say to me in the near future, "Are you happy now?" My answer to that question will probably be no. Although he will think that I am just never happy, I am always happy. I just always want to strive for happier. In the words of Jason, "When you need a little less or you want a little more…that's what I'm here for."

To meet Jason again may just have the same turn out, but right now I could have that experience everyday of my life and it would never get old. What is life without something to always look forward to? It would be boring if we always found complete satisfaction.

I am very satisfied with my everyday life, my husband and my family. I would not know what to do without them. As the realism of the fans world may seem a little crazy, it's always been my quirkiness.

As I was listening to the lyrics of my new Michael Castro downloads, I really found myself connecting to the lyrics, "There's no such thing as a perfect stranger." This is truly reality but it does not always change the way we fantasize. Although my real fantasies would be a "beautiful mistake," two people who really don't even know each other just laughing together is a beautiful reality.

I know that I will always have to put up with people, sometimes the ones who are the closest to me, always thinking that I'm a big weirdo, not really getting it. I am proud to know that I have no secrets and that this is just me. People will have to love me for who I am, take it or leave it.

I have no shame in the truths of being a fan. Any fan will tell you that there is nothing that keeps us going than the inspiration of the unknown, the exciting, or the impossible.

Regardless of what anybody says, there is no shame in reaching out to the stars. Whether it's a person who inspires us to dream a little, or a goal in which we dream to achieve great things.

2010
Jason Castro Red Room Cafe
Boston, MA

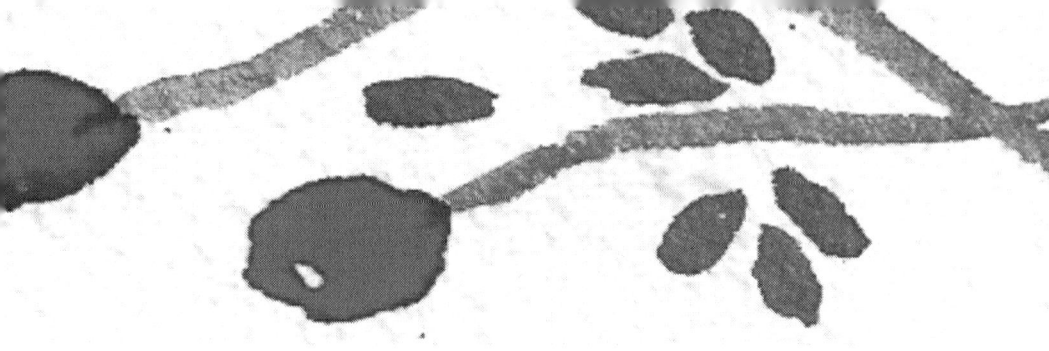

"It's only after someone is gone do you realize how much
you miss them."
~ Unknown

"Never regret. If it's good, it's wonderful.
If it's bad, it's experience."
~ Unknown

"Happiness comes of the capacity to feel deeply, to enjoy simply,
to think freely, to risk life, to be needed."
~ Anonymous

"Life is too short, Break the rules, Forgive quickly, Kiss slowly,
Love truly, Laugh uncontrollably, And never regret anything
that made you smile."
~ Unknown

"Everything happens for a reason, people change so you can
learn to let go, things go wrong so you can appreciate when
they are right, and sometimes good things fall apart so better
things can come together."
~ Marilyn Monroe

Chapter 21
Live & Learn: What Lies Beneath an
American Idol *Dream*

"Live and learn" is probably one of the most important and true clichés describing this journey called life.

I had a breakthrough today on this seventeenth day of November; the four year anniversary of my grandmother's passing. Her anniversary is technically on the eighteenth but just before midnight on the seventeenth, four years ago, I heard her speak to me, letting me know that she was alright. Therefore, personally, the day stands out to me more substantially.

During my daily two mile walk, which has been a recent priority since June, I was once again absorbed in lyrics while I was listening to my iPod. Sugarland's "Something More" seemed to summarize my life at the present moment, as I was still soul searching.

As my iPod continued to play, "Life don't go quite like you planned it, we try so hard to understand it, the irrefutable indisputable totally beautiful fact is…shit happens." *Sugarland*…isn't that the truth?

I was going through what I considered to be one of the most difficult times of my life. For a while, I had been feeling a lull in the excitement in my life. The fulfillment of my dreams came to a halt or a waiting game, and at the same time I was grieving the loss of a friend.

The night before, I went to bed and what started out as a vivid dream ended in awakening me from a terrible nightmare. The dream began with this man entering my life out of nowhere. I could not identify him other than the fact that he had amazing brown eyes and a pair of perfectly chiseled arms that were better than Danny Gokey's. He continually referred to me as "Sweet lips" and kept reminding me that he was drawn to my warm personality and that I made him "Smile." He drew me in with his eyes and through his expressions of feeling. He seemed to have an overwhelming control over me like I felt possessed when I was in or out of his presence. Our connection was strong and a feeling of happiness was guaranteed, deeper feelings overshadowing everything else going on around us at the moment. We enjoyed the simplicity of each other's company through a quick connection in personality, a mutual feeling of thinking we had known each other forever.

All of a sudden, like the flick of a switch, he went from looking at me with stars in his eyes to not looking at me at all. I had never showed myself to be anyone but someone who cared for him from beginning to end but on his end, it was like he was two different people. One who truly cared for me versus one who respected me so little as a person that he dismissed me instantly. It was like an emotional roller coaster. One moment I was on an unbelievable high and then I was in a downward spiral, out of control, suddenly running off the track, crashing and exploding.

I sat up in bed, real tears streaming down my cheeks with an actual feeling of true heartache, I couldn't understand the true meaning of this dream. In truth, there were several interpretations.

I started to revisit my whole purpose of who I am as a person and what I wanted out of life. I asked myself, "What is your goal?" Once again, I turned inward. I then realized at that very moment that there was more to my *American Idol* dreams than I was admitting... that what lies beneath those *American Idol* dreams may be a greater truth about the person I am, who I was and what I really wanted and or needed out of life. So what was at the root of it all?

As I was walking, feeling down by those three realizations; a lull in the excitement in life, a delay in the fulfillment of a dream, and grieving the loss of a friend through a betrayal. I then realized the dream I had was related to all three.

The dream started off with passion, a spark, a feeling of newness, excitement. All of those things that I spoke about that eventually disappear when you are in a long lasting relationship. What you are left with is the more important of the two but a lot of times women feel that they don't need the other piece, that they are content without it, or are they?

Had I been venting this missing piece that may be important to me through my idol obsessions? Was it all connected? I didn't know this person in my dream any better than I knew Clay Aiken or Jason Castro, both who at one time I had a strong physical attraction to which provided me with that passion and excitement that I craved

215

through fantasy. Were my idol obsessions and fantasies, masqueraded by musical ability through my passion for music, an outlet for that spark that was absent... something that you can never get back because it eventually fades in any relationship as things change?

The difference was that even though I created a fantasy in this dream, it was more like an actual reality. This person who I fell for was not a musician or even musically inclined and instead of indulging through a pair of hypnotizing blue eyes, I was absorbed in a seductive pair of brown eyes. I realized how easy it could be to replace my Jason Castro with an average Joe. Instead of a long awaited response from a fan letter, I was receiving mutual responses to mutual generated feelings where the safety and innocence was gone. This beautiful mistake actually scared me. I began to become more open minded about how things can happen and how easy it can be to get pulled into a situation, finding and channeling excitement through an unhealthy outlet without even knowing it. This is especially true for those people driven by feelings and heart. Situations are not always as black and white as people chose to see them. I realized how important it is to not be judgmental, unless you are perfect, and nobody is.

I realized that in any obsession there is something deep rooted that lies within a person that provokes these feelings. Everyone's experiences and reasons are different but it is all relevant. I realized that it is alright to have obsessions, as long as you realize what is at the root of it. If you are not aware of it, it can disrupt life as you know it and the things you hold dear to your heart.

I realized why the depression occurred whenever a concert was over due to the fact that the feeling of excitement ended and I never wanted it to. Maybe it was a blessing in disguise that I never really knew my idols, that "Sometimes we thank God for unanswered prayers," as spoken by Garth Brooks.

My interaction with Jason Castro was exactly what it should have been, no words exchanged and nothing involved but a simple feeling of excitement to be kept alive by not having it all the time.

In the time I signed a contract with an agent to move forward toward my dream of publishing a book, putting my dream at the tips of somebody else's fingertips with nothing but time on my hands, in those months I met a friend whom I lost four months later.

Like the dream, I was dealing with the loss of someone who I genuinely enjoyed in my life along with the acceptance of her betrayal as she found herself in an uncomfortable position in a particular situation.

Sometimes when you fear something enough it's easier to let another person take the fall because in humanity, people will go to extreme measures to protect that "something" that means the most to them. I knew what that was because she felt close enough to me to share those things and trust me with them.

I believe that sometimes in life, people will deal with a situation in the best way they know how and even though it may lack sense, everyone has their own way of reasoning and rationalizing.

There are also times in our life when we can look back on a situation and ask ourselves, *How could I fall for that or how could I be that naïve?* Then there are also times in our lives when we can distinguish between what was real from what was not because no one can be that good of an actress.

Along with the hurt and betrayal, I had to overcome the harsh reality that a person that I held in such high regard could actually be one of the weakest people I had ever met, and that inner strength substantially exceeds the physical strength of a person. It's called accountability, being honest, having enough character to admit that you're human and growing from experience.

I know that people come into our lives for a reason, a season, or a lifetime but what role did my friend play? Always having a habit of associating myself with people who were unhappy, and always wanting to save the world and need to be needed, I wondered if I felt that I needed to save my friend from her own unhappiness and that she needed me. In some respects, I think that was very true but I knew that was not the root of it. In truth, nobody can save the world, nor can you save a person who deep down is in fear of being saved.

I started to realize that every experience in life is a learning experience, good or unpleasant. I started to feel that maybe I could move forward by holding on to the good memories, never regretting anything that made me smile, and the unpleasant ones would eventually make me stronger. I guess everyone has to have a Judas in their life somewhere along the way. In accepting the fact that my friend will never be a part of my life, I wish her well in hers, as hurt and angry as I may be. Finding it difficult to heal from, it takes a minute to find a special person, an hour to appreciate them, a day to love them, but an entire life to forget them.

No truer words were spoken than these by Richard Back. "There are no mistakes. The events we bring upon ourselves, no matter how unpleasant, are necessary in order to learn what we need to learn, whatever steps we take, they're necessary to reach the places we've chosen to go."

This quote made me understand that my friend was a diversion. In the time I was waiting for someone else to make my dream come true, I got lost and traveled down a different path. One in which I needed to travel to come to the realization of who I am as a person and where I wanted to be in life. I was so far from whom I really was that I needed to take a step back, get back on track and learn that nobody was going to open doors for me. I needed to do it myself and this particular path pushed me toward reaching that goal and inspired me to take my unfortunate experience and make my dream a reality.

It is important in life to know that in following any dream that there will be diversions, people who set you off track, bumps in the road, a temporary source of happiness that may not be real or delay what is of greater importance. But the key to success is to never give up. Nobody is perfect and we are not supposed to be or we wouldn't be growing. It's important to follow your dreams because no matter where they take you, what is meant to be will be. You'll never know if you never try and then you will always live in wonder and maybe even in regret of passing up an opportunity for happiness.

I believe that in some people's lives there is more negativity than happiness. If this is true, they need to ask themselves, Am I really living my life or am I just going through the motions? In reality, if you're not really living, then you're dying. People should be happy in all aspects of their life. We create our own happiness and if we find ourselves in a place that is unhappy, it is because we chose to be there. Maybe the wake-up call is to make that change.

Some people are terrified of change. More importantly people should try not to fear it but to look it in the face, conquer it, live and grow. It is true that some people don't know who or where they want to be in life, but sometimes the best start is knowing who and where you don't want to be. Unfortunately, living in a world of denial, no matter what the circumstances are, is a destined path to never-ending unhappiness, solitude and emptiness.

Sometimes in life it is hard to not let others bring you down, but you can't. People who try to bring you down are usually not happy in their own lives. They are not strong enough to face truths and take a step toward that most needed change toward happiness. The most you can do is say a prayer that their lives will improve for them and concentrate on what is important in your own. It's important to be strong and hold yourself in high esteem no matter what anyone thinks or says.

There are dream weavers in life but there is also what we call dream crushers and unfortunately, they can even be the people who seem closest to you.

I thought good and hard about whom I really am as a person and what I wanted out of life because I am the creator of my own happiness. In taking stock of my life, I am lucky to have not only a husband by terms of marriage, but a companion and more importantly, a friend. In reality, I know that it is the strength of our solid foundation that can get us through anything.

If you can't say that your spouse is your best friend, the one who brings out the best in you, makes you feel important, someone who you look forward to spending time with, then maybe you haven't found your soul mate.

Someone once told me to make a list of all the things that I want to accomplish before my time is up, to keep life exciting and be a little crazy. Life is too short, and it is. It's important to have a wild side!

I think that after eight years of pondering about what was missing in my life, I realized the answer to that mystery was that nothing was missing at all. I came to a realization that I really didn't have a void in my life and that I have always had a happy life, but I am just always striving for happier. As I said, if we were always satisfied there would be nothing to look forward to. I think that in life we all at one point settle into a routine that becomes so every day for us that we begin to get a little bored. The key is to keep life exciting and stay young. For me, it's not that I need to have a life of fame. My passion just lies within a fascination through music and my love for singing and musical expression. I also have a passion for romance and fireworks. Sometimes when we are in a long lasting relationship with children and everyday responsibilities, it fades. I continue to find that excitement through my celebrity crushes, keeping in mind that is alright to create fireworks through fantasy rather than create a fantasy in something real.

My last online fortune cookie said, "Believe in yourself and you will be successful." I do believe in myself.

As far as my life goes, I am blessed to have many talents like playing guitar and expressing myself through voice. I will indulge in my music, especially if it is something that I can relate to whatever I am going through in my life at that moment.

I will have the self confidence to continue in my martial arts training.

I am thankful for my creativity and my generosity toward others.

Most of all, I am proud of my warm heart, which I have been accused more than once of wearing on my sleeve. This is who I am. It is a blessing that I have the amazing ability to love and even more than I should at times. Feeling is being human. Therefore, it is never wrong. At least I can say that if I die tomorrow, I don't have to worry about anyone not knowing how I felt about them. There is no greater honor than to be loved. Say what you feel and mean what you say, the quality of being genuine.

Instead of labeling people I don't care for in my life as insignificant, I will thank them for helping to make me that much stronger in realizing who I don't want to be and to take life to the next level, to stand proud and continue to be happy, alive and a free spirit.

It is a great compliment to be a jack of all trades, master of none. There is really no need to be a master of anything, better to dip into a little piece of everything. If you love yourself and the things you are doing, this is what attracts others. People like to be around happiness, not those who bring them down.

In the past few days, I received the death card on my Facebook page. This card represents the beginning of a new life as a result of underlying circumstances transformation and change; the end of a phase in life that has served its purpose. I believe in this as much as I live by my daily horoscope and my ability to fulfill the role of a lioness which is a zest for life with a warm spirit, deeply sensual and passionate, open-hearted, creative, enthusiastic, independent, confident and generous. Leo's despise dull and regular routines and create their own excitement.

So I live for new excitement in my life, and when I get bored, I search for something new. There is nothing wrong with that. Even if I need to sometimes create a little fantasy, imagining what it would be like to walk on the red carpet, the excitement of writing a fan letter and hoping for a response, going to a concert and experiencing a rush, a simple trip to Mohegan Sun or the still dream of appearing on the Ellen DeGeneres Show.

I imagine it all like this, as in Miley Cyrus' song:

> *"I hopped off the plane at LAX*
> *with a dream and my cardigan*
> *welcome to the land of fame excess,*
> *am I gonna fit in?*

Jumped in the cab,

Here I am for the first time

Look to my right and I see the Hollywood sign

This is all too crazy

Everybody seems so famous

My tummys turning and I'm feelin kinda home sick

Too much pressure and I'm nervous,

That's when the taxi man turned on the radio

And a Britney song was on

So I put my hands up

They're playin my song,

And the butterflies fly away

Noddin' my head like yeah

Moving my hips like yeah,

And I got my hands up,

They're playin my song

I know I'm gonna be ok

Yeah, it's a party in the USA!"

I am fully aware that moment could recreate itself with me standing on the giant ottoman at the front of our sectional singing into a hairbrush, but who cares. Every small moment of passion that we find ourselves relishing in is relevant in creating a lifetime of positive energy. Music, expression through lyrics, the thoughts of performing and dancing on an episode of *Glee*, meeting a star and fantasizing about the feeling I get when I look into his eyes, and the opportunity to love or be loved. These are my passions and my happy places.

It is important to have goals and dreams and it is even more important to follow them in some way or another. If there is a void or lull in excitement in your life, make it a goal to fill that void or to create that excitement. Follow a dream, and if it seems too far from your reach, fill the void and create excitement with another source of happiness. Create a healthy fantasy, find a fun loving hobby, explore your wild side and where your passion lies. In the wise words of an unknown author, "Someday your life will flash before your eyes, make sure it's worth watching."

Everyone's dreams and ideas of excitement are different but it's all relevant. Keeping the excitement alive inside of us is where we all find happiness. Life is not only what lies on the surface but what lies beneath an *American Idol* dream.

Made in the USA
Charleston, SC
17 July 2012